JANE AUSTEN'S CHRISTMAS

THE FESTIVE SEASON IN GEORGIAN ENGLAND

Jane Austen

JANE AUSTEN'S CHRISTMAS

THE FESTIVE SEASON
IN GEORGIAN ENGLAND

Researched and compiled by

MARIA HUBERT

SUTTON PUBLISHING

First published in the United Kingdom in 1996
Sutton Publishing Limited · Phoenix Mill · Thrupp
Stroud · Gloucestershire

British Library Cataloguing in Publication Data
A catalogue record for this book is available from the British Library

ISBN 0-7509-1307-X

™ ALAN SUTTON™ and SUTTON™ are the
trade marks of Sutton Publishing Limited

Typeset in 11/15 Sabon.
Typesetting and origination by
Sutton Publishing Limited.
Printed in Great Britain by
Ebenezer Baylis, Worcester.

CONTENTS

Christmas at Mansfield Park

Jane Austen

Set at the home of Sir Thomas and Lady Bertram, Mansfield Park, and spanning several Christmas seasons, the gentle romantic comedy of that name gives tantalizing glimpses of a Christmas we are never quite a party to. Would that Miss Austen had seen it fit to describe the 'Christmas Gaieties' which Miss Crawford refers to in a one-liner, when she asks Fanny about a letter received: 'Was his letter a long one? – Does he give you much account of what he is doing? – Is it the Christmas Gaieties that he is staying for?' The 'He' is, of course, Fanny's cousin, Edmund, who intent on his own life is no longer joining the seasonal family gathering, when young Fanny Price visits Mansfield Park; but as with all good romances, she wins her man in the end despite the apparent lack of Christmas spirit!

Amid the cares and complacency which his own children suggested, Sir Thomas did not forget to do what he could for the children of Mrs Price; he assisted her liberally in the education and disposal of her sons as they became old enough for a determinate pursuit: and Fanny, though almost totally separated from her family was sensible of the truest satisfaction in hearing any kindness towards them, or of anything at all promising in their situation and conduct. Once and only once in the course of many years, had she the happiness of being with William. Of the rest she saw nothing; nobody seemed to think of her ever going amongst them again, even for a visit, nobody at home seemed to want her; but William determining, soon after her removal, to be a sailor, was invited to spend a week with his sister in Northamptonshire, before he went to sea. Their eager affection in meeting, their exquisite delight in being together, their hours of happy mirth, and moments of serious conference, may be imagined; as well as the sanguine views and spirits of the boy even to the last, and the misery of the girl when he left her. Luckily the visit happened over the Christmas holidays, when she could directly look for comfort to her cousin Edmund; and he told her such charming things of what William was to do, and be hereafter, in consequence of his profession, as made her gradually admit that the separation might have some use. Edmund's friendship never failed her . . . she loved him better than anybody in the world except William; her heart was divided between the two.

Some time later, when Fanny is fifteen years old, she is with Sir Thomas's family hoping for the promised return of her brother after some six years.

The winter came . . . the accounts continued perfectly good; – and Mrs Norris in promoting gaieties for her nieces, assisting their toilettes, displaying their accomplishments, and looking about for their future husbands, had so much to do as, in addition to her own household cares, some interference in those of her sister, and Mrs Grant's wasteful doings to overlook, left her very little occasion to be occupied even in fears for the absent . . . Fanny had no share in the festivities of the season; but she enjoyed being avowedly useful as her aunt's companion, when they called away the rest of the family; and as Miss Leigh had left Mansfield, she naturally became everything to Lady Bertram during the night of a Ball or a Party . . . As to her cousin's gaieties, she loved to hear an account of them, especially of the balls, and whom Edmund had danced with; but though too lowly of her own situation to imagine she should ever be admitted to the same, and listened therefore without an idea of any nearer concern in them. Upon the whole it was a comfortable winter to her; for though it brought no William to England, the never failing hope of his arrival was worth much.

The next Christmas event sees not only the beloved brother William home, but Fanny preparing to go to the ball.

William's desire to see Fanny dance made more than a momentary impression on his uncle . . .

'I do not like, William, that you should leave Northampton without this indulgence. It would give me pleasure to see you both dance. You spoke of the balls at Northampton. Your cousins have occasionally attended them but they would not altogether suit us now. The fatigue would be too much for your aunt. I believe we must not think of a Northampton ball, a dance at home would be more eligible, and if ——'

'Ah! My dear Sir Thomas,' interrupted Mrs Norris, 'I knew what was coming. I knew what you were going to say. If dear Julia were at home, or dearest Mrs Rushworth at Sotherton, to afford a reason, an occasion for such a thing, you would be tempted to give the young people a dance at Mansfield. I know you would. If they were at home to grace a ball, a ball you would have this very Christmas. Thank your uncle, William, thank your uncle.' . . .

The ball began. It was rather honour than happiness to Fanny, for the first dance at least; her partner was in excellent spirits and tried to impart them to her, but she was a great deal too much frightened to have any enjoyment, til she could suppose herself no longer looked at. Young, pretty, and gentle, however she had no awkwardnesses that were not as good as graces, and there were few persons present that were not disposed to praise her . . .

Shortly afterwards, Sir Thomas was again interfering a little with her inclination, by advising her to go immediately to bed. 'Advise' was his word,

The Dance, by Randolph Caldicott

but it was the advice of absolute power, and she had only to rise and, with Mr Crawford's very cordial adieus, pass quietly away; stopping at the entrance door, like the Lady of Branxholm Hall, 'one moment and no more', to view the happy scene, and take a last look at the five or six determined couples, who were still hard at work – and then, creeping slowly up the principal staircase, pursued by the ceaseless country-dance, feverish with hopes and fears, soup and negus, sorefooted and fatigued, restless and agitated, yet feeling, in spite of everything, that a ball was indeed delightful . . .

Cousin Eliza's Christmas Gaieties

Elizabeth Hancock was the daughter of Tysoe and Philadelphia, her mother being Jane Austen's aunt. She married a French count, Jean Capotte, from whom she gained the title of Madame Comtesse de Feuillide. Jean was guillotined in 1794, and Eliza later married one of Jane's brothers, Henry, with whom she had long flirted.

The following is a letter from the early days of Eliza's marriage to the Count de Feuillide, to her cousin Philadelphia Walter, the Walters being half-cousins on Jane's maternal side. 'Philly' had written several letters, including her Christmas letter telling about her attendance at a ball, but none seemed to arrive in France. Eliza was obviously so taken up with the combined social events of the birth of a new baby for the King and Queen and the festive social scene that it was March (1782) before she wrote, but she describes the winter's festive season balls and fashions very well.

Elizabeth de Feuillide to Philadelphia Walter, Paris, 27 March 1782

I should never have the courage to address my dear cousin Philly, if I had not the greatest confidence in her friendship, and the greatest desire to convince her that I have never ceased to think of her with real affection; I am nevertheless not altogether so blameable as I may appear to be, as I did not receive your letter till long after its date owing to the neglect of servants, and my being out of town. As to the two former epistles you mention they never came to my hands; I imagine a letter I wrote you a short time before my marriage must likewise have been lost, as you speak of not having heard from me for above a twelvemonth; this would imply a neglect which I can never be guilty of where you are concerned, for be assured my dear cousin, you can have no friend more sincerely attached to you than myself and neither time nor absence can affect the regard I have ever felt for you.

The accounts which your letter brought me of the health and welfare of you and yours gave me infinite pleasure . . . I doubt not that you will wish I should give you some account of myself. My Uncle Austen acquainted you with my marriage soon after its taking place. This event, the most important one of my life, was you may imagine the effect of a mature deliberation . . . The man to whom I have given my hand is in every way amiable both in mind and person. It is too little to

The trials of fashionable dressing. A contemporary drawing of a lady's boudoir in the early nineteenth-century Book of Fashionable Etiquette

say he loves me, since he literally adores me; entirely devoted to me, and making my inclinations the guide of all his actions.

I enjoy . . . the advantages of rank and title, and a numerous and brilliant acquaintance . . .

In your last you gave me a description of a ball you had been at, I suppose you have been to more than one since. It is an amusement you seem to be fond of, and I doubt not but you have reason to be so, as I daresay you never go into publick without being distinguished. You mention your desire of being well dressed. It is a very natural one and usual to young persons as I know by experience. I have since my marriage endeavoured to find out some pretty silk which I might send you for a gown, as I have long wished to give my dearest Cousin this small mark of my regard but the not knowing exactly your taste and the great difficulty and risk of sending unmade silk has at last induced me to beg you to accept a draft on Mr Hoare, Mamma's Banker and which she will put into my letter in its stead. You may in this manner make purchase of what is most agreeable to you. I hope my dear Philly will not be offended at this freedom . . .

As for me, I have danced more this winter than in all the rest of my life put together. Indeed I am almost ashamed to say what a racketing life I have led, but it was really almost unavoidable, Paris has been remarkably gay this year on account of the birth of the Dauphin. This event was celebrated by fireworks, illuminations, balls etc. The entertainment of the latter kind given at court was amazingly fine. The Court of France is at all times brilliant, but on this occasion the magnificence was beyond conception. The ball was given in a most noble saloon, adorned with paintings, sculptures, gilding etc. etc. Eight thousand lights disposed in the most beautiful forms shewd to advantage the richest and most elegant dresses, the most beautiful women, and the noblest Assembly perhaps anywhere to be beheld; nothing but gold, silver, diamonds and jewels of all kinds were to be seen on every side. Her Majesty, who is handsome at all times, had her charms not a little heightened by the magnificence of her adjustment. It was a kind of Turkish dress made of a silver grounded silk intermixed with blue and entirely trimmed and almost covered with jewels. A sash and tassels of diamonds went round her waist, her sleeves were puffed and confined in many places with diamonds, large knots of the same fastened a flowing veil of silver gauze; her hair, which is remarkably handsome, was adorned with the most beautiful jewels of all kinds intermixed with flowers and a large plume of white feathers.

The king had a gold grounded coat entirely embroidered with jewels, the Comte d'Artois and the princesses were dressed with equal magnificence, and persons of the court by no means fell short of them. In short altogether it was the finest sight I ever beheld, and I cannot give you a better idea of it than the one which struck me at the time, which was this: it answered exactly to the description given in the Arabian Nights entertainments of enchanted palaces.

Besides this ball we had many others, but luckily for me they are now nearly over, as so much dancing, altho' perfectly to my taste, does not agree quite so well with my health, which tho' pretty good is not strong, that is I am seldom or ever ill, but my constitution is naturally delicate. I hope to spend the summer quietly . . .

A Pianoforte for Christmas

One of the earliest Christmas references to the Austens' Christmas is a short but descriptive letter from Mrs Austen to her niece Philadelphia Walters, whose father was also a clergyman, and their living at Seal in Kent. Her mother seems to have kept her away from the wicked world and very much under her thumb; Phila was a country girl, backward in fashionable living, and decidedly prim. She shows, in her several letters, jealousy and prudish disapproval of both her cousin Eliza and of Jane Austen. It would appear that the pianoforte mentioned in this letter may have been borrowed just for the family party, though Jane refers in one of her later letters to the fact that she plays, so presumably the family subsequently acquired a piano of their own.

Illustration from the Macmillan original Mansfield Park, *1895*

Steventon, 31 December 1786

. . . We are now happy in the company of our Sister Hancock, Madame de Feuillide and the little boy; they came to us last Thursday Sennet and will stay with us till the end of next month. They all look and seem to be remarkably well, the little boy grows very fat, he is very fair and very pretty; I don't think your aunt is at all alter'd in any respect, Madame is grown quite lively, when a child, we used to think her too grave. We have borrowed a pianoforte and she plays for us every day; on Tuesday we are to have a very snug little dance in our parlour, just our own children, nephew and nieces, (for the two little Coopers come tomorrow) quite a family party. I wish my third niece could be here also; but indeed I begin to suspect your mother never intends to gratify that wish. You might as well be in Jamaica keeping your Brother's house for anything that we see of you or are likely to see. Five of my children are now at home, Henry, Frank, Charles and my two Girls, who have now quite left school; Frank returns to Portsmouth in a few days, he has but short holidays at Christmas. Edward is well and happy in Switzerland, James set out for La Guienne, on a visit to the Count Feuillide, near Eight weeks ago, I hope he is got there by this time and am impatient for a Letter; he was wind-bound for some weeks in the little island of Jersey or he would have got to the end of his long journey in the beginning of this Month. Every one of our fireside joins in Love and Duty as due and in wishing a happy 87 to our dear friends at Seal.

Unfashionably Prudish

A MYSTERY FOR CHRISTMAS

*Christmas tradition includes, unfortunately, a fair amount of family
tension even in the best families: magazines from the eighteenth century to
the present are full of helpful advice on how to deal with such problems.
The Austen family was, it seems, no exception. The following Christmas
drama evolves from the letters and journal entries written between Eliza,
Jane's aunt (Eliza Comtesse de Feuillide), and her prim and proper cousin,
Philadelphia Walters, sometimes called Philly or Phila, whose mother was
largely responsible for her prudish ways.*

*The story begins in the autumn of 1787. Eliza came to England to
have her baby and spend some time with her mother in London. Baby
Hastings was born and Eliza hit the social scene almost immediately,
spending a season at Tunbridge Wells with her mother and cousin, Phila.
Phila was not happy at first, as she writes to her brother James.*

For the first days I was miserable, and would have given anything to
get away to any retired corner, but their great kindness, affection
and attention to me soon reconciled me to the dissipated life they led
and put me in mind that every woman is at heart a rake . . . I will just
relate a few of the particulars from my Journal.

We all left Seale at 5 o'clock the 6th inst. in
an elegant coach and four, as they seldom stir
without, got to the Wells and went directly
to the Rooms for the benefit of two
celebrated Italian singers: after they had
done singing some gentleman proposed
dancing which was readily agreed to and we
kept it up till past twelve.

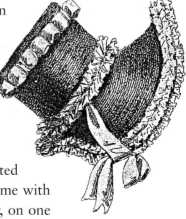

On Friday morning the Comtesse and I hunted
all the Milliner's shops for hats: she presented me with
a very pretty fancy hat to wear behind the hair, on one

The Rectory at Steventon

side, and as a mixture of colours is quite the thing, I chose green and pink with a wreath of pink roses and feathers; but the taste is for all the most frightful colours. Her dress was new . . . most truly elegant, quite distinguished as the richest in the Rooms – I danced almost all the evening and kept it up till past two o'clock concluding with a French Dance . . . 'The Bakers Wife', only six couples and in the Cotillon style, the figure changing every time. We danced it full an hour and half.

The account continues with stories of theatregoing, a day at the races, card games and more balls. Phila's praise of her aunt Eliza is very high, and not at all in keeping with the impression some biographers have of her being of a peevish and jealous nature.

They were very desirous of keeping me longer with them as they had some thought of going for a week to Brighton and wished me to be of the party, but I declined it upon my mother's account.

They go at Xmas to Steventon and mean to act a play 'Which is the

Man' and 'Bon Ton.' My uncle's barn is fitting up quite like a theatre and all the young folks are to take their part. The Countess is Lady Bob Lardoon in the former and Miss Tittup in the latter. They wish me much of the party and offer to carry me, but I do not think of it. I should like to be a spectator, but am sure I should not have the courage to act a part, nor do I wish to attain it: its agreed I am to spend some time with them in Town after Xmas: they do not go abroad till Spring.

Could it be that Phila really did, at heart, want to be part of the play, but her upbringing and her natural lack of self-confidence held her back? Or was she afraid of reprisals from her mother, who probably disapproved of the fact that her daughter was dancing and dining every night at Tunbridge, and requested her return to Seal? Phila does make mention of the fact that she did not go on to Brighton with the party because of her mother. Also, her mother had refused to allow her to spend the previous Christmas with the Austens at Steventon. This must have been hard for a young lady of nineteen.

Despite the most enjoyable time she owed to Eliza, Phila became more 'dog in the manger' upon being pressed further to join the Christmas party, so that her letters become very impolite for the times. Eliza, not used to being denied, was equally determined to have the company of the niece she loved so much, with endorsement from Mrs Austen who herself had failed to elicit Phila's mother's permission for the girl to spend Christmas at Steventon on several occasions.

Eliza to Philadelphia, 16 November 1787

. . . I have a favour to ask of you my dear Friend, a favour which I trust you will not refuse me. You know we have long projected acting this Christmas in Hampshire and this scheme would go on a vast deal better would you lend your assistance. You may remember when you was at Tunbridge my expressing a very earnest and natural wish to have you with me during the approaching festival, and on finding there were two unengaged parts I immediately thought of you, and am particularly commissioned by my aunt Austen and her whole family, to make the earliest application possible, and assure you how very happy you will make them as well as myself if you could be prevailed upon to undertake these parts and give us all your company . . . I know you have engagements but if you love me put them off to another year; consider it is the only Christmas we may pass together for many many years, whereas you have it always within your power to be with your other friends, who I am sure are too reasonable to object to your taking this only opportunity of being with an affectionate relative from whom the sea will very soon divide you. As to any diffidence in regard to succeeding in the parts . . . I assure you they are neither long nor difficult, and I am certain you will succeed in them . . . Do not let your dress neither disturb you as I think I can manage it so that the Green Room should provide you with what is necessary for acting. We purpose setting out the 17th December, so that if you can come to us in Orchard Street the day before, I shall be happy to have you go down with me, and when once the plays are over, if you are determined to quit us, we will consent however reluctantly to part with you. I assure you we shall have a most brilliant party and a great deal of amusement, the house full of company and frequent balls. You cannot possibly resist so many temptations, especially when I tell you your old friend James is returned from France and is to be in the acting party.

Phila's reply, which was full of apparent excuses about leaving her mother alone, other engagements, and the fact that she felt it wrong to 'appear in public with male actors in sexual embraces', provoked a stern reply from the usually affectionate and bubbling Eliza, whose annoyance at her cousin's stubbornness shows in the way she emphasizes her words.

Orchard Street, 23 November 1787

. . . I need not tell you how much I am concerned at your not being able to comply with a request which in all probability I shall never have it in my power to make again. The not leaving your Mother alone is certainly very essential, but would it not be possible to engage some Friend or Neighbour to come and stay with her during so short an absence? I will only allow myself to take notice of the strong reluctance you express to what you call <u>appearing in publick</u>. I assure you our performance is to be by no means a publick one, since only a select party of friends will be present.

Part of her letter was considered so improper for the time that it was not published complete until 1942 (according to her biographer, Park Honan). Certainly the letters privately published by the Leigh-Austen family, and presented to the Bath Reference Library in the 1890s, do not include the phrases in Honan, which refer to the fact that Eliza is surprised and hurt that Phila would believe she would press her to do anything in an 'improper or disadvantageous light'. Phila may have also committed the social blunder of slapping down the invitation, by asking the minimum time she would be required – as if it were a trial rather than a pleasure – which obviously caused much offence:

You wish to know the <u>exact time</u> which we should be satisfied with, and therefore I proceed to acquaint you that a fortnight from New Years Day <u>would do</u>, provided however you could bring yourself to act, for my aunt Austen declares 'she has not room for any <u>idle</u>, <u>young</u> people'.

Eliza also seems to think that the mother is behind Phila's reticence, as these blunt remarks reveal:

Shall I be candid and tell you the Thought that has struck me on the occasion? – the insuperable objection to my proposal is, some scruples of your mother's about acting – if this is the case I can only say it is a Pity so groundless a prejudice should be harboured in so enlightened and enlarged a mind.

This letter appears to have brought no response at all, and the party and theatricals at Steventon went on without the presence of Miss Walters. It looks as if the aunts and cousins felt that the life of Phila was not proceeding along the right lines for the times, and they were united in an attempt to prise her away from her clinging mother, so that she might enjoy some time with people her own age.

A St Nicholas Verse

Jane Austen

Throughout Europe, England being no exception, the custom of giving a gift on 6 December, in commemoration of St Nicholas, was widespread. Eventually, however, separate customs tended to become condensed. Thus a gift given for New Year or Twelfth Night also often had a verse attached. The following verse by Jane Austen was attached to a gift of a little Gingham needle bag made for a departing friend in January 1792.

> This little bag, I hope, will prove
> To be not vainly made;
> For should you thread and needles want,
> It will afford you aid.
>
> And, as we are about to part,
> 'Twill serve another end:
> For, when you look upon this bag,
> You'll recollect your friend.

Britannia's Housewives Blithe

Romaine Joseph Thorne

A clever play on words for the Christmas season, written in 1795. The italics and capitals are within the original poem, and may indicate that it was a game of some kind, such as were most popular in the eighteenth century.

CONVIVIAL SEASON! At thy near approach
In *country towns*, Britannia's HOUSEWIVES, blithe,
Their *pewter*, *brass* and *tin* utensils scour:
Their *windows* too, they by ablution rid
Of spot opaque; and much their cleansing *brush*,
In every secret cranny of the house,
Annoys the *spider* tyrant of the walls!
And deals destruction to his curious webb.
Well pleas'd, their store of fam'ly *plate* they take
From *cupboard* lock'd, where, haply it hath stood
A period long, by all the household train
Untouch'd, unseen; but, now, is burnish'd up
(To dignify th'approaching festive hours,
And gaily entertain expected friends)
In brightness equal to the radient shield
Which careful THETIS, anxious for the weal
Of great ACHILLES, to the hero gave.
From ev'ry hedge is pluck'd by eager hands
The HOLLY BRANCH with prickly leaves replete,
And fraught with berries of a crimson hue;
Which, torn asunder from its parent trunk,
Is straightway taken to the Neighb'ring towns,
Where *windows*, *mantels*, *candlesticks*, and *shelves*,
Quarts, *pints*, *decanters*, *pipkins*, *pasons*, *jugs*,
And other articles of household ware,
The verdant garb confess.

Or if to *forfeits* they the sport confine,
The happy folk, adjacent to the fire,
Their stations take; excepting one alone
(Sometimes the social mistress of the house)
Who sits within the centre of the room,
To cry the *pawns*: much is the laughter now,
Arising slowly from the aukward lot
As such as can't the *Christmas catch* repeat,
And who, perchance, are sentenc'd to salute
The jetty beauties of the *chimney-back*,

Or *lady's shoe*; others, more lucky far
By hap, or favour, meet a sweeter doom,
And, on each fair-one's lovely lips imprint
The ardent *kiss*; blushing, the maiden, coy,
With fruitless strength, endeavours to resist
The am'rous youth, and shun his warm embrace;
Whilst, fir'd with transport, he pursues the bliss,
Nor rests till the pleasing task complete.

The Norfolk Stagecoach bringing turkeys to London, by R. Seymour

Charades for Christmas

In 1895 there appeared an anonymous private booklet of the charades and theatrical conundrums written by the Austen family for their own entertainment. This offers yet another glimpse of the delightful Christmases the Austens enjoyed in their home, particularly at Steventon. Charades remained popular right into the 1960s when they suddenly disappeared from the family Christmas entertainment, possibly because of the lack of numbers present. They are simply three-act plays, each one describing a syllable of a word.

The game was played one of two ways. First, it could be a relaxed parlour game, whereby everyone could stay seated. Each player in turn would recite their conundrum, and the rest had to guess at the word. Alternatively, the party would divide into two or more groups, and having decided on their word, they would create short one-minute acts to describe the syllables, the last describing the whole word. The word had to be said in the act. An example of these charade plays appears later in this book (p. 30). Here is the short discourse about the Austen charades from the book.

It is not as a celebrated writer that she appears in these pages, but as one of a family group gathered round the fireside at Steventon Rectory, Chawton Manor House, or Godmersham Park, to enliven the long evenings of a hundred years ago by merry verse and happy, careless inventions of the moment, such as flowed without difficulty from the lively minds and ready pens of those among whom she lived.

Three of these charades are by Jane herself, and even if her name did not appear beneath them, their authorship might possibly have been apparent to those already acquainted with the playful exaggerations and sparkling nonsense in which she sometimes loved to indulge when writing with perfect unrestraint to her sister and other relations. In all works intended for the public eye these had to be kept within due bounds; we find nothing but the soberest decorum in the charade laid long ago upon the table at Hartfield, and transcribed by Emma into that thin quarto of hot pressed paper which Harriet was making, 'her only mental provision for the evening of life'.

The habit of writing charades seems to have been general in the Austen family. Only one by her father survives, and to that the answer is unknown; but there are several by her mother, Cassandra Leigh by birth, who was well gifted with – to use a term of her own – 'sprack wit'. Cassandra's brother James Leigh, who inherited the estate of North Leigh in Oxfordshire from the Perrots, and added their name to his own, was noted in the family as a good writer of charades, and four of his lead the way in this little collection. They may have been composed by him in his young days in Bath, in which gay and fashionable resort he and his wife were often to be found, or at his country home, Scarlets, in Berkshire, where as an older man he passed most of his time.

All the other charades come from the pens of three generations of Austens, and are inserted according to the ages of the writers . . . from her parents to a nephew, who being nearly nineteen at the time of her death in 1817, and well able to use his pen by that time, can claim a place among the Steventon writers.

Here are the three charades by Jane herself, preceded by two by James Leigh Perrot, illustrated by Miss Hill – reproduced for the first time since 1895! The answers are to be found at the back of the book (p. 120), so no cheating!

No. III

In confinement I'm chained every day
Yet my enemies need not be crowing
To my chain I have always a key,
And no prison can keep me from going.

Small and weak are my hands I'll allow,
Yet for striking my character's great,
Though ruined by one fatal blow,
My strokes, if hard pressed, I repeat.

I have neither mouth, eye nor ear
Yet I always keep time as I sing,
Change of season I never need fear
Though my being depends on the spring.

Would you wish, if these hints are too few
One glimpse of my figure to catch?
Look round! I shall soon be in view
If you have but your eyes on the watch.

No. IV

Though low is my station
   The Chief of the Nation
      On me for support oft depend;
         Young and old, strong and weak,
           My assistance all seek,
             Yet all turn their backs on their
             friend.

             At the first rout in town
             Every Duchess will own,
              My company not a
              disgrace;
              Yet at each rout you'll
              find
              I am still left behind,
             And to everyone forced to
             give place.

             Without bribe or treat,
            I have always a seat
           In the Chapel so famed, of St
          Stephen;
          There I lean to no side,
          With no party divide,
         But keep myself steady and
      even.

        Each debate I attend,
       From beginning to end,
     Yet I seem neither weary nor weaker;
In the house every day
Not a word do I say,
Yet in me you behold a good Speaker.

No. XVIII

When my first is a task to a young
                    girl of spirit,
And my second confines her to
                    finish the piece,
How hard is her fate! But
        how great is her merit,
If by taking my all she
                    effects her release!

No. XIX

Divided, I'm a gentleman
In public deeds and powers;
United I'm a monster, who
That gentleman devours.

No. XX

You may lie on my first by the
                    side of a stream,
And my second compose to the
                    nymph you adore,
But if, when you've none of my whole, her esteem
And affection diminish – think of her no more!

Lady Susan Spoils Christmas

Jane Austen

Lady Susan is a little-known story written by Jane Austen in 1805. It was not published until 1871. Jane's earliest attempts at writing appear to be in the form of letters. In the following extract the invitation to spend Christmas is declined on the grounds that Lady Susan is to visit, and may, it would seem from the tone of the letter, overstay her welcome.

Letter 3 Mrs Vernon to Lady de Courcy, Churchill

My dear Mother,

I am very sorry to tell you it will not be in our power to keep our promise of spending our Christmas with you; and we are prevented that happiness by a circumstance which is not likely to make us any amends. Lady Susan in a letter to her Brother has declared her intention of visiting us almost immediately – and as such a visit is in all probability merely an affair of convenience, it is impossible to conjecture its length. I was by no means prepared for such an event, nor can I now account for her Ladyship's conduct. Langford appeared so exactly the place for her in every respect, as well from the elegant and expensive stile of Living there, as from her particular attachment to Mrs Manwaring, that I was very far from expecting so speedy a distinction, tho' I always imagined from her increasing friendship for us since her Husband's death, that we should at some future period be obliged to receive her. Mr Vernon I think was a great deal too kind to her when he was in Staffordshire. Her behaviour to him, independent of her general Character, has been so inexcusably artful and ungenerous since our Marriage was first in agitation, that no one less amiable and mild than himself could have overlooked it at all; and tho' as his Brother's widow and in narrow circumstances it was proper to render her pecuniary assistance, I cannot help thinking his pressing invitation to visit us at Churchill perfectly unnecessary. Disposed however as he always is to think the best of every one her display of Grief, and professions of regret and general resolutions of prudence were sufficient to soften his heart, and make him really confide in her sincerity. But as for myself, I am still unconvinced; and plausibly as her Ladyship has now written, I cannot make up my mind, till I better understand her real meaning in coming to us. You may guess therefore my dear Madam, with what feelings I look forward to her arrival. She will have occasion for all those attractive powers for which she is celebrated, to gain any share of my regard; and I shall certainly endeavour to guard myself against their influence, if not accompanied by something more substantial. She expresses a most eager desire of being acquainted with me, and makes very gracious mention of my children, but I am not quite weak enough to suppose a woman who has behaved with inattention if not unkindness to her own child, should be attached to any of mine. Miss Vernon is to be placed at a school in Town before her Mother comes to us, which I am glad of, for her sake and for my own. It must be to her advantage to be separated from her Mother; and a girl of sixteen who has received so wretched an education would not be a very desirable companion here. Reginald has long wished I know to see this captivating Lady Susan, and we shall depend on his joining our party soon. I am glad to hear that my Father continues so well, and am, with best Love etc.,

Cath. Vernon

Letter 13 Lady de Courcy to Mrs Vernon, Parklands

My dear Catherine,

Unluckily I was confined to my room when your last letter came, by a cold which affected my eyes so much as to prevent my reading it myself, so I could not refuse your Father when he offered to read it to me, by which means he became acquainted to my great vexation with all your fears about your brother. I had intended to write to Reginald myself as soon as my eyes would let me, to point out as well as I could the danger of an intimate acquaintance with so artful a woman as Lady Susan, to a young Man of his age and high expectations. I meant moreover to have reminded him of our being quite alone now, and very

A Poem for Christmas Day 1795
Robert Southey

This poem was written on Christmas Day.

How many hearts are happy at this hour
In England! Brightly o'er the cheerful hall
Flares the heaped hearth, and friends and kindred meet,
And the glad mother round her festive board
Beholds her children, separated long.

Amid the world's ways, assembled now,
A sight at which affection lightens up
With smiles, the eye that age has long bedimm'd.

I do remember when I was a child
How my young heart, a stranger then to care,
With transport leap'd upon this holyday,
As o'er the house, all gay with evergreens,
From friend to friend with joyful speed I ran,
Bidding a merry Christmas to them all.

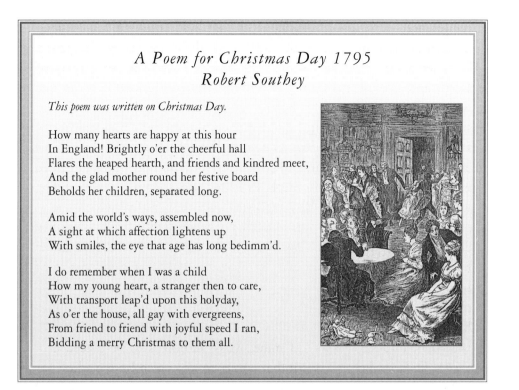

much in need of him to keep our spirits up these long winter evenings. Whether it would have done any good, can never be settled now; but I am excessively vexed that Sir Reginald should know anything of a matter which we forsaw would make him uneasy. He caught all your fears the moment he read your Letter, and I am sure has not had the business out of his head since; he wrote by the same post to Reginald, a long letter full of it all, and particularly asking an explanation of what he may have heard from Lady Susan to contradict the late shocking reports. His answer came this morning, which I shall enclose to you, as I think you will like to see it; I wish it was more satisfactory, but it seems written with such a determination to think well of Lady Susan, that his assurances as to Marriage etc. do not set my heart at ease. I say all I can however to satisfy your Father, and he is certainly less uneasy since Reginald's letter. How provoking it is my dear Catherine, that this unwelcome Guest of yours, should not only prevent our meeting this Christmas, but be the occasion of so much vexation and trouble. Kiss the dear Children for me. Your affec: Mother

C. de Courcy.

Dances and Charities

On Christmas Eve 1798 Jane Austen writes to her sister Cassandra to describe the seasonal ball.

I spent my time [at Manydown] very quietly and very pleasantly with Catherine. Miss Blanchford is agreeable enough. I do not want people to be very agreeable, as it saves me the trouble of liking them a great deal.

Our ball was very thin, but by no means unpleasant. There were thirty-one people, and only eleven ladies out of the number, and but five single women in the room. Of the gentlemen present you must have some idea from the list of my partners, Mr Wood, G. Lefroy, Rice, a Mr Butcher (belonging to the Temples, a sailor and not of the 11th Light Dragoons), Mr Temple (not the horrid one of all), Mr Wm Orde (cousin to the Kingslere man), Mr John Harwood and Mr Calland, who appeared as usual with his hat in his hand, and stood every now and then behind Catherine and me to be talked to and abused for not dancing. We teased him, however, into it as last. I was very glad to see him again after so long a separation, and he was altogether the genius and flirt of the evening. He enquired after you.

There were twenty dances, and I danced them all without any fatigue. I was glad to find myself capable of dancing so much, and with so much satisfaction as I did; from my slender enjoyment of the Ashford Balls (as assemblies for dancing) I had not thought myself equal to it, but in cold weather and with few couples I fancy I could just as well dance for a week together as for half an hour. My black cap was openly admired by Mrs Lefroy, and secretly, I imagine, by everybody else in the room.

Tuesday. I thank you for your long letter, which I will endeavour to deserve by writing the rest of this closely as possible. I am full of joy at much of your information; that you should have been to a ball and have danced at it, and supped with the Prince, and that you should meditate the purchase of a new muslin gown, are delightful circumstances. I am determined to buy a handsome one whenever I can, and I am so tired and ashamed of half my present wardrobe which contains them. But I will not be much longer libelled by the possession of my course spot; I shall turn it into a petticoat very soon. I wish you a Merry Xmas but no compliments of the season.

Poor Edward! It is very hard that he, who has everything else in the world that he can wish for, should not have good health too . . . I know no one more deserving of happiness without alloy than Edward is.

I cannot determine what to do about my new gown; I wish such things were to be bought ready-made. I have some hopes of meeting Martha at the christening at Deane next Tuesday, and shall see what she can do for me. I want to have something suggested which will give me no trouble of thought or direction.

Again I return to my joy that you danced at Ashford and that you supped with the Prince. I can perfectly comprehend Mrs Cage's distress and perplexity. She has all those kind of foolish and incomprehensible feelings which would make her fancy herself uncomfortable in such a party. I love her however, in spite of all her nonsense. Pray give 't'other Miss Austen's' compliments to Edward Bridges when you see him again.

Of my charities to the poor since I came home, you shall have faithful account. I have given a pair of worsted stockings to Mary Hutchins, Dame Kew, Mary Steevens and Dame Staples; a shift to Hannah Staples, and a shawl to Betty Dawkins; amounting in all to about half a guinea. But I have no reason to suppose that the Batty's would accept of anything, because I have not made them the offer.

Muslin for a New Gown

The matter of new gowns was of great importance to young ladies who frequented the same balls and assemblies week after week – especially in the more fashionable resorts and houses. Jane's letters refer frequently to the purchase of muslin, cambric or some other fashionable material wherewith to make a gown, dress a hat, etc. No doubt such advertisements as the following one by Mr S. Slack in the December issue of a Bath newspaper in 1804 were read most eagerly, and pennies counted out for the forthcoming purchase.

. . . with the greatest respect to inform Ladies, &c. of his return from attending the East India Company's sales in London, where he hath purchased the most Extensive Collection of every Description of INDIA MUSLINS ever offered for sale in the city.

From the advantage of purchasing with ready money, the moderate profit charged on each piece, and the great variety he can shew, will, he flatters himself, be the means of securing him that presence he hath so liberally experienced for these five years past.

Ladies who take whole pieces or half pieces will have a very considerable allowance made. A quantity of elegant work'd muslins and shawls brought as presents from India.

Striped Muslins at *2s* & *2/6d* per yard. A quantity of yard and half wide mulls at *2/6d* & *3/-* per yard, lately sold at *5/6d* . . .

BRITISH MUSLINS &c. – Very good Japan Muslin at *15s* a dress, handsome patterns at *20s*, 300 elegant work'd dresses in sprigs and colonades, equal in appearance to India. 200 British Cambrics at *12s* per

Georgian engraving showing a dress of the period

piece . . . Cambric Muslins of a new manufacture, warranted to retain their colour, and will be sold cheap. Also, dimities, calicos, White Ginghams &c.

Jane Austen writes to Cassandra in celebratory mood on 28 December 1798:

My Dear Cassandra,

Frank is made! He was yesterday raised to the rank of Commander and appointed to the Petterel sloop, now at Gibraltar . . . This letter is dedicated entirely to good news . . . if you don't buy a muslin gown on the strength of this money and Frank's promotion, I shall never forgive you!

And again, in January 1801, after mischievously commenting that the Christmas festivities at Godmersham, which her sister Cassandra was then extolling, would have even satisfied their pretentious cousin Philadelphia Walters, she continues:

I am glad that the Wildmans are going to give a Ball, and hope you will not fail to benefit both yourself and me, by laying out a few kisses in the purchase of a frank. – I believe you are right in proposing to delay the Cambric Muslin, and I submit with a kind of voluntary reluctance.

Later in the same letter, Jane refers in her usual blunt way to guests at a dinner she attends:

Martha and I dined yesterday at Deane to meet the Powletts and Tom Chute, which we did not fail to do. Mrs Powlett was at once expensively and nakedly dress'd; we have had the satisfaction of estimating her Lace and her Muslin; and she said too little to afford us much other amusement.

Thankfulness and Sauce

R e v d   W i l l i a m   H o l l a n d

Revd Holland was a West Country parson in the late eighteenth–early nineteenth centuries. For much of his parochial life he kept a diary of the daily events of his parish; the Christmas entries give us an idea of how a country clergyman such as Jane Austen's father might have passed the festive season. In these entries for 1799 he comments on the poor, who traditionally came for charitable gifts at Christmas time.

Monday 23 December 1799
Butter very scarce and Robert went out to seek some. Though it froze so hard that scarce any creature could stand yet forsooth he took the great horse, and against my will too. He will rot with laziness by and by. The poor came for meat and corn this cold weather and against Christmas Season. Some very thankful and some almost saucy.

Tuesday 24 December 1799
Much harried by the poor of the parish who come for Christmas Gifts. Many persons rather in affluence came but this is not right because it takes from those who are real objects. The Lower Classes have no pride of this kind among them, and the Somerset Lower Classes less of this Pride than any other.

The Festive Board

In Jane's England, the Christmas holidays lasted for several weeks, due in part to the tedious journeys undertaken to visit family for the holidays, and the quite obvious fact, from several of her novels as well as from her own letters, that guests were reluctant to leave again! This put a strain on the cook and housewife alike, and a varied and full menu had to be prepared for guests, and for the possibility of those same guests being snowbound, and not being able to depart.

The Austen's friend and cook, Martha Lloyd, kept a book of such delights. The friendship probably began in 1789, when Jane's father let Deane Parsonage to the widow of a Welsh parson. Mrs Lloyd's daughters and the Austen girls became good friends, and Martha eventually went to live with the Austens in 1792, when the parsonage was claimed by James Austen, a curate at Overton, and she later married Francis Austen, at the tender age of sixty-two!

The Austens could not afford the luxury of a fine French chef, such as the one kept by their brother at Godmersham. When their mother's health failed, Jane and her sister Cassandra shared the task of housekeeper. Jane particularly enjoyed what she termed 'experimental housekeeping', and Martha brought out this enjoyment with her own love of cooking, and the collecting of recipes from friends.

Martha kept her recipes in a leather-bound book. The recipes must have evoked memories of the occasions at which the meals were eaten, such as the Christmas in Southampton in 1808, which Jane wrote about to Cassandra, then staying at Godmersham with their brother, a tedious party delayed by the late arrival of some of their guests, and which lasted from 'seven o'clock until eleven o'clock . . . The last hour spent yawning and shivering in a wide circle round the fire was dull enough.' The company, which seems to have included two elderly ladies, must have been duller still, 'but the tray had admirable success. The widgeon and the preserved ginger were as delicious as one could wish. But as to our Black Butter, do not decoy anybody to Southampton by such a lure for it is all gone.'

This celebrated Black Butter does not appear in any of Martha's writings, nor anywhere else, other than a scanty description of their own unsuccessful attempt to make the confection. It may have been introduced to the family, living as they did in Southampton, by means of a seafaring friend. It is well known on the continent, where it has been made by housewives for centuries, as a healthy winter preserve. Or they may have got it from much farther afield. The following recipe for Black Apple Butter comes from the Pennsylvanian Dutch, who took the recipes with them from Holland to the New World in 1734. It is served at Thanksgiving in commemoration of the

Pease soup recipe, handwritten by Martha Lloyd

voyage, and would have been a novel recipe indeed which one of the Austen's wide circle of seafaring family and friends might have brought them.

> *Take 4 pounds of full ripe apples, and peel and core them. Meanwhile put into a pan 2 pints of sweet cider, and boil until it reduces by half. Put the apples, chopped small, to the cider. Cook slowly stirring frequently, until the fruit is tender, as you can crush beneath the back of a spoon. Then work the apple through a sieve, and return to the pan adding 1 lb beaten (granulated) sugar and spices as following, 1 teaspoon clove well ground, 2 teaspoons cinnamon well ground, 1 saltspoon allspice well ground. Cook over low fire for about ¾ hour, stirring until mixture thickens and turns a rich brown. Pour the butter into small clean jars, and cover with clarified butter when cold. Seal and keep for three months before using. By this time the butter will have turned almost black, and have a most delicious flavour.*

The family's own attempts to make this delicacy seem to have been less than successful; as Jane told her sister, the results were only fit to be eaten in 'unpretended privacy'.

The brawn of old England, a remnant of the boar's head, was still very popular in Jane's time. It was known as both brawn and souse, which was a pickled version. The Austen's farm produce at Steventon included pigs, which made brawns as well as many other tasty meat portions suitable for feeding any number of seasonal house-guests from the Christmas larder. Soused in a strong brine in November, the brawns would keep well as a cold table repast to serve right through the season to Twelfth Night. In a letter written as late as 14 January (1796), Jane says, 'Caroline, Anna and I have just been devouring some cold Souse, and it would be difficult to say which enjoyed it most.' It is mentioned as part of the feast laid out at Uppercross, with the 'trestles and trays bending under the weight of brawn and cold pies . . . the whole completed by a roaring Christmas fire'.

While mutton held pride of place on many an eighteenth-century Christmas table, and was the Christmas Eve dish served roasted to John Knightley in the novel *Emma*, venison was the socially acceptable meat for the very wealthy. To have venison showed that one had sufficient parklands to graze the deer, thus it was a high status symbol. The deer park of Jane's brother's estate at Godmersham served the table at Rowling, where Jane ate her venison in 1796. She uses the socially supreme habit of eating the meat in *Mansfield Park*, and serves it to Mr Darcy in *Pride and Prejudice*. The master of Northanger Abbey also boasts of his gift of half a buck to his club.

The now very popular turkey was well known to the Austens who in fact bred the birds. At an end of season ball, probably for a belated Twelfth Night party on 8 January 1796, Jane relates that her brother James 'cut up the Turkey with great perseverance', and later, in 1812, Jane wrote to Martha Lloyd asking for an address of one acquaintance, Mr Morton, to whom she wished to send a Christmas gift of a turkey.

The Christmas goose, however, was not so Christmassy in Georgian and Regency times, it being more popular at Michaelmas in September, which was the time of the goose and hiring fairs. At this time, young geese had always been sold at market to fatten up for Christmas, and the hirelings would present themselves at the same markets to be taken on by a new employer. It was said that to eat goose on Michelmas ensured good financial luck; 'He 'at eateth goose on Michelmas won't find his pockets short of brass' was the Yorkshire version of the old saying. Jane Austen wrote to Cassandra on Michaelmas 1813, 'I dined upon Goose today, which I hope will secure a good Sale of my 2nd edition.'

The Turkey Stage

Peter Parley

*A Regency storyteller's amusing tale (from Parley's
Tales about Christmas, 1828).*

Every traveller had a holiday appearance; there were an unusual number
of caravans, wagons and vehicles of all kinds, the coaches were
unmercifully loaded, and the coachmen had an air of more than common
importance. One stage coach could scarcely get up a chalky hill that it had
to ascend, though six horses were attached to it, so heavy was the pile of
hampers, baskets, packages, and parcels piled on the roof. Mr Charlton said
that it reminded him of once seeing the Norfolk Turkey Coach, so loaded
with turkeys, that it ought to have been called the Turkey Stage. There was

*'I should hardly have been surprised to see a turkey or two, running after the coach . . .
screaming out that their places had been booked three days before'*

scarcely anything to be seen but turkeys, so piled was the outside of the coach, and so crammed the inside, that they wanted nothing in the world but a Turkey for a Coachman, and another for a guard to render the thing quite complete.

'I should hardly have been surprised', added he, 'to see a turkey or two, running after the coach, labelled round the neck, "for Leadenhall Market", and screaming out that their places had been booked three days before.'

The Invalids' Christmas

Revd   William   Holland

Further entries from the West Country parson's diary.

Sunday 20 December 1801

Sent off Morris with a note to Mr Blake at Asholt to inform him that Mr Eyton will do the Duty there. In the meantime I prepared myself for the Service at this Church. I was carried to Church in an armed chair. Mr Wm Frost with his broad back on one side and Mr Amen with his unsound leg on the other and Master Morris with his spruce Livery and spindle shanks behind. The shrivelled leg and spindle shanks had nearly given way, I called for assistance when Lo, a stout young Morle advanced and so I got safe to the Porch and walked into Church. I went thro' the Duty very well but few at Church the day very uncomfortable.

Wednesday 23 December 1801

A very wet nasty morning. We breakfasted tolerably early for invalids. My wife's finger somewhat easier but it is still in an unpleasant way. Margaret a little better. My gout considerably better. William running up and down stairs like a Buck. Sent the Clerk and Morris with the barley to the maltster to be wetted tomorrow. Wrote a letter to Wm Tutton and received a facetious letter from the Duke of Somerset. The Poor of the Parish begin to come round for Christmas gifts.

Friday 25 December 1801

The Singers at the window tuned forth a most dismal ditty, half drunk too and with the most wretched voices. The day very rainy and uncommonly unpleasant. I got myself ready for Church and at last sallied forth with my feet well surrounded with flannel. I did the Duty very well and we had a Sacrament. I had a chair and carpet within the Rails being obliged to sit down often to rest my legs. After this I had Mr Woodhouse's horse and Morris rode the great horse and we sallied forth like Don Quixote and his man Sancho for Asholt. I got safe to Asholt and got out of my Gambadoes.* It was very wet from the Churchyard Gate to the Church and the Church itself quite wet with damp. The little Clerk was quite glad to see me. I asked whether I was not to have him to dine with me. He said that he had ten children come to see him and he had them to dine with him. Ho said I thats another thing, indeed he seemed pretty well laden already. It rained on my return very hard but Morris had got an umbrella for me and so with my Gambadoes and two greatcoats I was a match for the weather where I found a full house, having no less than ten persons to dine in the kitchen. I trust and hope this day's business has not hurt me. A day of labour but I have got through it very well I think.

* *Gambadoes are leather boots attached to the saddle.*

Georgian Christmas Puddings

Christmas pudding as we now know it first appeared in the reign of King George III. It was said to have been invented especially for him by his chef, because of his inordinate love of English puddings. Before this, the pudding was more of a pottage or porridge, with all the right ingredients we tend to associate with the traditional Christmas pudding, but cooked in a large cloth, and rather sloppy!

A rather amusing recipe in rhyme, written by Mrs Austen for Martha Lloyd's Receipt Book, sounds very much like Christmas pudding, and may well have served as such in the Austen household, especially as the last verse refers to two being made, one to be served 'out of season'. Only a Christmas pudding could be put out to serve, then taken away and survive reboiling! Also, the line 'And more savoury things if well chosen' seems to refer more to the ingredients of the early Christmas pudding than to any other sort.

If the Vicar you treat
You must give him to eat
A pudding to his affection,
And to make his repast
By the canon of taste
Be the present receipt your direction.

First take two pounds of bread
Be the crumb only weigh'd
For the crust the good housewife refuses,
The proportions you'll guess,
May be made more or less
To the size the family chuses.

Then its sweetness to make;
Some currants you take,

And sugar, of each half a pound,
Be not butter forgot
And the quantity sought
Must the same as your currants be found.

Cloves and Mace you will want
With Rose Water I grant,
And more savoury things if well chosen.
Then to bind each ingredient
You'll find most expedient
Of eggs to put in half a dozen.

Some milk, don't refuse it
But boil as you use it,
A proper hint for its maker.
And the whole when compleat
With care recommend the baker.

In praise of this pudding,
I vouch it a good one,
Or should you suspect a fond word,
To every guest,
Perhaps it is best
Two puddings should smoke on the board.

Two puddings! yet – no,
For if one will do
The other comes in out of season;
And these lines but obey,
Nor can anyone say
That this pudding's without rhyme or reason!

Puddings of all kinds were particularly popular dishes prepared, presumably, to fill with the least expense the many stomachs of the constant flow of seasonal house visitors traditional during the Georgian Christmas season, which could last from early December until after Twelfth Night,

6 January. In a letter to Cassandra on 7 January 1807, Jane's relief at the departure of the Christmas guests is obvious, yet tinged with a little Christian regret, as befits a proper clergyman's daughter.

When you receive this our guests will all be gone or going; and I shall be left to the comfortable disposal of my time, to ease of mind from the torments of rice puddings and apple dumplings, and probably to regret that I did not take more pains to please them all.

The following recipe for Festive Rice Pudding is from Martha's book. No wonder it was deemed fit to serve at polite gatherings and Christmas parties. John Knightley and his sons were going home to their 'hot roasted Mutton and Rice Puddings' in *Emma*, with some enthusiasm.

Six ounces of rice flour, one quart of cream. Mix it well together and boil it; put it to half a pound of butter, and half a pound of sugar and one nutmeg grated and then take it off [the heat]. When cold, beat six egg whites and all and put it to it: butter your dish before you put it in. Bake it quick, and you may paste your dish if you please.

Some eighteenth-century recipes made this dish with a cover of sweet thin pastry before putting it into the oven.

A Parlour Theatrical

Jane Austen

The following little one-act play turned up in a scarce book of Jane Austen juvenilia compiled by G.K. Chesterton in the nineteenth century. From the names of the characters, and its style, it was possibly written as a Christmas entertainment by the young Jane, perhaps for Twelfth Night. Here it is in its entirety.

THE FIRST ACT OF A COMEDY
Characters

Popgun	Maria
Charles	Pistoletta
Postilion	Hostess
Chorus of ploughboys	Cook
and	and
Strephon	Chloe

SCENE – AN INN

Enter Hostess, Charles, Maria, and Cook.

Hostess to Maria	If the gentry in the Lion should want beds, shew them number 9.
Maria	Yes Mistress.— *exit* Maria.
Hostess to cook	If their Honours in the Moon ask for the bill of fare, give it them.
Cook	I wull, I wull. *exit* Cook.
Hostess to Charles	If their Ladyships in the Sun ring their Bell – answer it.
Charles	Yes Madam. *Exeunt* Severally.

SCENE CHANGES TO THE MOON, AND DISCOVERS
POPGUN AND PISTOLETTA.

Pistoletta	Pray papa how far is it to London?
Popgun	My Girl, my Darling, my favourite of all my Children, who art the picture of thy poor Mother who died two months ago, with whom I am going to Town to marry to Strephon, and to whom I mean to bequeath my whole Estate, it wants seven Miles.

SCENE CHANGES TO THE SUN

Enter Chloe and a chorus of ploughboys.

Chloe	Where am I? At Hounslow.—Where go I? To London—. What to do? To be married—. Unto whom? Unto Strephon. Who is he? A Youth. Then I will sing a song.

SONG

I go to Town
And when I come down,
I shall be married to Streephon*
And that to me will be fun.

Chorus   Be fun, be fun, be fun,
And that to me will be fun.

Enter Cook
Cook   Here is the bill of fare.
Chloe reads   2 Ducks, a leg of beef, a stinking partridge, and a tart.—I will have the leg of beef and the partridge.
exit Cook.

And now I will sing another song.

SONG

I am going to have my dinner,
After which I shan't be thinner,
I wish I had here Strephon
For he would carve the partridge
if it should be a tough one.

Chorus   Tough one, tough one, tough one
For he would carve the partridge if it
Should be a tough one.
Exit Chloe and Chorus.—

SCENE CHANGES TO THE INSIDE OF THE LION
Enter Strephon and Postilion.

Streph   You drove me from Staines to this place, from whence I mean to go to Town to marry Chloe. How much is your due?
Post   Eighteen pence.

---

* Note *the two e's.*

Streph	Alas, my friend, I have but a bad guinea with which I mean to support myself in Town. But I will pawn to you an undirected Letter that I received from Chloe.
Post	Sir, I accept your offer.

END OF THE FIRST ACT

The Cold in this Country is Intense . . .

Robert Southey

One of Jane Austen's favourite books was Robert Southey's Letters from England, *published in 1807. Purporting to be an observation of English custom and manner written by a Spanish visitor to English shores, and translated into English from the Spanish, it was in fact written by Southey himself. Letter number 58 covers all aspects of the Christmas season and begins with an observation about winter weather in England.*

2 January 1803

'If you would live in health,' says the proverb, 'wear the same garment in summer that you wear in winter.' It seems as if the English had some fool's adage by the little difference there is between their summer and their winter apparel. The men indeed, when they go abroad put on a great coat, and the women wear muffs and fur around the neck; but all these are laid aside in the house, I no longer wonder why these people talk so much of the weather; they live in the most inconstant of all climates, against which it is difficult to take any effectual precaution, that they have given the matter up in despair and take no precautions at all . . .

'Why do you not warm your rooms like the Germans,' I say to them, 'and diffuse the heat equally on all sides?'

'Oh,' they reply, 'it is so dismal not to see the fire!' And so for the sake of seeing the fire, they are contented to be half starved and half roasted at the same time, and to have more women and children burnt to death in one year than all the heretics who ever suffered in England in the days when heresy was thought a crime.

I happened to sleep in the country when the first snow fell; and in the morning when I looked out of the window, everything was white, and the snowflakes like feathers floating and falling with as endless and ever varying motions as the dance of mosquitos on a summer evening. And this mockery of life was the only appearance of life; and indeed it seemed as if there could be nothing living in such a world. The trees were clothed like the earth, every bough, branch, and spray; except that side of the bark which had not been exposed to the wind, nothing was to be seen but was perfectly and dazzling white; and the evergreens in the garden were bent by the load. White mountains in the distance can give no idea of this singular effect. I was equally delighted with the incrustation upon the inside of the windows. Nothing which I have seen equals the exquisite beauty of this frost work. But when I returned to London the scene was widely different. There the atmosphere is so full of soot from the earth-coal, that the snow is sullied as it falls; men were throwing it from the roof of every house by shovels full, lest it should soak through the roof; – and when it began to melt the streets were more filthy and miserable than I could have conceived possible. In wet weather women wear a clog, which is raised upon an iron ring about two inches from the ground; they clatter along the streets like horses.

The cold in this country is intense; and because it is not quite severe enough to nip off a man's nose if he puts it out of doors, they take no precautions against it, and therefore suffer more than the Germans or the Russians. Nay, the Russian soldiers who were in England during the late war died of the cold; they had been accustomed to their furs and their stoves, for which regimentals and English barracks were such bad substitutes, that they sickened and died off like rotten sheep. Liquids freeze in the house. My water bottle burst last night with a loud report.

I happened to go into a pastrycook's shop one morning, and inquired of the mistress why she kept her window open during this severe weather – which I observed most of the trade did. She told me that were she to close it, her receipts would be lessened by forty or fifty shillings a day – so many were the persons who took up buns or biscuits as they passed by and threw their pence in, not allowing themselves time to enter. Was there ever so indefatigable a people! Some of the English sweetmeats exceed ours; the currant and the raspberry, fruits which flourish in a cold climate, form delicious preserves. Their iced creams are also richer than our iced waters; but these northern people do not understand the management of southern luxuries; they fill their cellars with ice instead of snow, though it is procured with more difficulty and greater expense, and must be broken to the consistency of compressed snow before it can be used.

Bullet Pudding and Messy Games

What is Bullet Pudding? Is it a family name for Christmas Pudding, or the name given to a particular pudding which turned out hard as a bullet? Has it anything to do with Christmas at all, in fact? Certainly it was a mystery to Miss Chapman who was the recipient of Fanny Austen's letter in which she describes the Twelfth Night party at her brother Edward's seat, Godmersham Park in Kent (for Fanny and Miss Chapman, see p. 51). However, here is Fanny's letter, with mention of the mysterious Bullet Pudding, then her explanation following Miss Chapman's confessed ignorance of the dish. The account of the Twelfth Night game of drawing character cards is well described here too.

Godmersham Park, 8 January 1804

My Dear Miss Chapman,
As it is a long while since we have heard of one another, I think you will not be sorry to have a letter from me. I have so many things to tell you that I do not know where to begin. In the first place you will be glad to hear that Brothers came home in good health and spirits 21st of last month. We have all spent a very merry Christmas and I hope you have also. We had different amusements every evening. 1st we had Bullet Pudding, then Snap Dragon. In the evening we dance or play at

The daring game of 'Snapdragons', by R. Seymour

cards. The day before yesterday we drew King and Queen and drew such funny names you cannot think! I was Suky Sweetlips, Edward – John Bull, George – King, Henry – Little Jack Horner, William – Little Tom Thumb, Elizabeth – Polly Primrose, Marianne – Goody Twoshoes, Mama and Papa – Margery Mutton Pie and Johnny Bo-Peep, Aunt Louisa – Queen, and Aunt Harriet – Dorothy Do-little. The King and Queen sat upon two high thrones and held a Levee . . . The whole concluded with a nice game at Commerce in which John Bull won the pool; I hope this minute account of Twelfth-day will amuse you, I suppose you likewise drew King and Queen. If you did I shall like very much to know some of the names, particularly yours. You will be surprised to hear that Miss Sharpe is not yet come she has been dangerously ill poor thing . . .

Mama desires her compliments to you and thinks it is a long while since we have heard from you which we hope to do soon. Sackree [?] desires her best respects to you and wishes you a happy new year. Pray have you been to any balls lately? perhaps you were at the last Feversham Ball which we hear was a very good one. The other day I was very much surprised to see your Brother's marriage in the paper for I thought it was all over the 100 years . . . Today the men are to appear in there cloaths for the first time. Captain Austen looks very nice in his red coat, blue breeches, and red sash, he is now sitting opposite to me and I can hardly write my letter for looking at him. The hat is a plain round common one with an oak bough and a crescent in the middle. If I had more room I might tell you something else but as I have not I must conclude with best love from all of us.

Snapdragon – which involves popping raisins into the mouth from a bowl of flaming brandy – is a delightful pastime, popular from the sixteenth century or even earlier, which we still have at Christmas festivities in our family.

Godmersham Park, 17 January 1804

My Dear Miss Chapman,

I take the first opportunity of thanking you for the nice letter and beautiful purse you were so good as to send me. I like it very much as does everybody who has seen it. I was surprised to hear that you did

Godmersham Park

not know what a Bullet Pudding is, but as you don't I will endeavour to describe it as follows:

You must have a large pewter dish filled with flour which you must pile up into a sort of pudding with a peek at top. You must then lay a bullet at top and everybody cuts a slice of it, and the person that is cutting it when it falls must poke about with their noses and chins till they find it and then take it out with their mouths of which makes them strange figures all covered with flour but the worst is that you must not laugh for fear of the flour getting up your nose and mouth and choking you: You must not use your hands in taking the Bullet out. I wish you success with your Lottery ticket. I have one also . . .

Since I wrote the above Papa has had a letter to say that my Ticket is drawn a prize of £20 and as he is going to Canterbury today I have begged him to get me another which I hope will at least be as lucky a one as the last.

Last night we had a pail of water and an apple which as you may suppose delighted the little ones. Think of me Monday for that is the day of our Fete . . .

We all join in best love to you
Yrs Affec.
Fanny Catherine Austen.

PS excuse bad writing.

Fanny's reference to the pail of water and the apple is, of course, to the old game of apple-bobbing, which often took place after the country custom of Wassailing the Orchards. Yet another messy game this, with an apple bobbing around on water, which participants have to catch with their mouths and take a bite from!

The Parson at Work and Play

R e v d   W i l l i a m   H o l l a n d

Contrasting entries from the West Country parson's diary.

Thursday 13 December 1804

About 4 o'clock a chaise came from Bridgwater and my wife and I with Margaret and the two Miss Lewis went off. We reached Mr Jenkin's School some time before the play begun. There was a good deal of bustle getting the young actors ready. The play was Othello or the Moor of Venice, Mr Gill's Writing Room as the theatre and very well fitted out it was. The speeches begun first among the younger ones. In popped my little boy William who was the youngest of them all but spoke as well as any of them and was much clapped. Then the play begun. Young Blake did the part of Othello, the two Stradlings acted Desdemona and Amelia and two prettier girls I scarce ever saw insomuch that some said it was a pity they should be boys.

The Preacher, by Randolph Caldicott

One Giles acted the part of Iago, a tall awkward looking young man. All the dresses were very proper and Desdemona's head was covered with diamonds. The room was very hot and all was conducted very regularly. A boy dressed like an Orange Girl came with a basket to take the tickets and most gave half a crown, I gave half a guinea. We had a very pleasant and satisfactory jaunt and we got into bed before two in the morning.

Wednesday 25 December 1806

A very rainy day. I issued out this morning to go to Asholt but the rain soon came on in a torrent like manner and well it was for me that I had an umbrella. I got safe and administered the Sacrament to ten persons, pretty well for Asholt. Returned through great rain yet preserved by my umbrella. I found at home the persons who dwelt in the Cottages where William was taken when he fell from his horse, and there was a large party in the kitchen. Robert, an old servant and some of our neighbours. We went to Church first and I had a Christening afterwards and a Sacrament in the morning and two Sermons and heavy rain and uncomfortable weather. It was altogether fatiguing. After dinner we called in the wives of the Inhabitants of the Cottage who came to see William and made an additional present of half a Guinea each to them for their Care, Kindness and Humanity and invited them to dine here every Christmas Day in Future. They seemed much pleased with the notice taken of them. They went off before supper in a very tempestuous night and had some three miles to go. Some of the party staid later and some till after supper. Robert, an old servant of mine, and now a respectable chandler seemed growing fat apace. At last they all made their bow and we soon tripp'd off for bed.

Saturday 24 December 1808

A hard frosty morning and a good deal of snow on the ground. After breakfast the poor poured in for corn and my wife was very busy. Dyer is here carrying out dung, or rather ashes, to the Moors. Miss Hartwell dined here today and we had hare to dinner which we have not very often tho I am qualified to kill game and we have game around us, yet not having taken out a Licence I do not go out and no one sends me game, at least not often tho this hare was sent me by Mr St Albyn. I cannot think Government take such a very large sum by this Act and it is hard that qualified persons should not be allowed to have their amusement without restraint. As to the unqualified they in fact cannot in general afford to idle their time away in this manner.

Sunday 25 December 1808

This is Christmas Day and the frost very severe. Few at Church and few at the Sacrament. I had some bad spasms while doing Duty and with difficulty got through the Duty yet I persevered. We had several persons of our neighbours to dine in the kitchen. They left us about five o'clock and then the evening was spent in the usual way of Sundays.

Monday 26 December 1808

I read Prayers this morning. We had a few at Church and a Christening and a Churching. Gave George leave to keep a holiday, he is gone on a visit with his father. When I got out of Church I found young Southcomb here from Rose Ash in Devon. He is at Allen's of Bridgewater from Tiverton School, a nephew of Mrs Southcomb's Husband. A very plain young man and a madness in the family. William asked one of the young Hartwells to dine here and they have been firing little brass cannons all morning.

Tuesday 27 December 1808

Snow fell in the night. Both Margaret and William disappointed in not being able to go to the Ball in Bridgewater, nor even to Enmore as they intended, it being a hazy morning and the snow very high. George had a holiday yesterday but he came early in the morning and I have since sent him for coal as I concluded the roads must be beaten along the Turnpike and towards Combych. William has been all morning making a large snowball and has curiously hollowed the inside and placed a candle in it and got some black paper with eyes, nose and mouth cut in it which at night will look tremendous. When night came on it did appear somewhat strange and terrible.

Thursday 29 December 1808

This morning too very dismal and foggy, my face tho somewhat better. The frost is quite gone, even William's hollow ball in the garden is almost entirely vanished. About 2 o'clock a horse was brought from Mr Ling for Mr Southcomb who is to dine here today in his way to Stowgumber. He came, but not till half an hour after time. (A curious Genius I think). However he dined here and so did the servant but he's left his horse to be sent back to Bridgewater by the Post tomorrow and taken Mr Ling's horse to go to Stowgumber and the man not much pleased marches off on foot. After this my wife, self and William played at Five Card Loo.

Friday 30 December 1808

I have been poorly with a nervous agitation and Spasms in my face. Dyer is here in the barn. I promised to go over with William to Enmore but feel myself almost unequal to the undertaking yet my wife seems to think a little society may do me good. So after a good deal of resolving and unresolving I, covered with two great coats and my faithful woolen network around my face, moved off and William on his little poney, neatly trimmed, with me. We had a good deal of rain and passed along that awful road at Pikeley where William fell, and in short got safe to Enmore where we found old Mrs Poole better a good deal than she has been. Margaret too I found well, and the Divine and his sister Charlotte. There we dined and there we staid the night. William was my bedfellow this night and now and then he moved about a little unplesantly.

'This is Christmas Day and the frost very severe . . .', by Randolph Caldicott

Gaieties and Masques at Godmersham Park, 1806

Jane's elder brother Edward was adopted by a distant relative, Thomas Knight, who owned a stately pile in Kent, Godmersham Park. Sir Thomas had no direct heir. Edward took the name Knight, and inherited the park. His daughter, Fanny, kept diaries for sixty-eight years about life at Godmersham, and wrote long delightfully descriptive letters to her family and friends all about the events, the balls and parties at her family home, which seemed to glitter from one season to the next with social gatherings of one sort or another – a sharp contrast to the festivities of the Austens.

Fanny also kept up a long correspondence, from 1803 to 1857, with Miss Dorothy Chapman, her ex-governess. In the following letter, Fanny describes minutely the Christmas 1806 season at her family home, giving a wonderful insight into the Georgian Christmas festivities at a large country house. (For the full explanation of the Twelfth Night masquerade, see pp. 87–9. For the games Snapdragon, Bullace Pudding (Bullet Pudding) and Apple in Water, see pp. 43–6.)

Godmersham Park, 12 January 1806

My dear Miss Chapman,

I am much obliged to you for your letter which I am afraid you will have thought me a long while in answering, but really I have been so much taken up with amusements lately and having had Fanny Cage here likewise, I have not been able to find time before. I do not think that you have been at all long in executing my commission and therefore no apologies are necessary. I believe the enclosed is what I am indebted to you for it, if it is not enough, you will tell me when you write. I have spent a most delightful Christmas indeed, and as you are so good as to enquire about it, I will give you an account of some of our amusements. In the first place, soon after Christmas-day, Aunts Louisa and Harriet, Uncles Edward and John and Uncle H. Austen came, not forgetting Fanny and Sophia Cage, so we had a fine party you see for any kind of fun. On Saturday 4th we all acted a delightful play, or select piece. If I had a frank I would send you a playbill, but as I have not, you must e'en go without it, and be contented with my description of it. It was unknown to everybody except to Papa and Mama, and it all went of uncommonly well. Miss S. was our manager, and without her we could have done nothing. Mama was our Musician, all the servants were invited to see us, and the company sat by the curtains in the breakfast parlour, so we had a very good stage. Miss Sharpe contrived the dresses and they were admirable! nothing could be better suited. First George repeated a prologue, then came 'Alfred, A Drama', then an appropriate address by Lizzy; 'Pride

Painting of Fanny by her aunt, Cassandra Austen

punished – or Innocence rewarded', a little piece of Miss Sharpe's.

Duchess – George; Flora, a shepherdess – F. Cage; Fairy Serena – myself; The prologue to Barbarossa – Edward; The 1st. scene . . . Act of Douglas; Lord Randolph G.; Norval – E; Lady R. – myself; the whole concluded with 'The Cits Country Box' by Fanny Catherine Austen. I forgot 'The Fairy's own' . . . by Lizzy, next to 'Pride punished'. It was a delightful evening, and everybody seemed pleased.

On Twelfth day we were all agreeably surprised with a sort of masquerade, all being dressed in character, and then we were conducted into the library, which was all lighted up and at one end a throne, surrounded with a grove of Orange Trees, and other shrubs, and all this was totally unknown to us all! Was it not delightful? I should have liked you very much to have been of the party. Now I will tell you our different characters. Edward and I were a Shepherd King and Queen; Mama a Savoyarde with a Hurdy-Gurdy; Marianne and William her children with a Tambourine and Triangle; Papa and Aunt Louisa – Sir Bertram and Lady Beadmasc one hundred years old – Aunt L with a great hoop; Aunt H a Pilgrim; Uncle John – a Turk; Uncle H. Austen – a Jew; Uncle E – a Jewess; Miss Sharpe – a Witch; Elizabeth – a flowergirl; Sophia – a fruitgirl; Fanny Cage – a Haymaker; George – Harlequin; Henry – Clown; and Charley a Cupid! Was it not a good one for him, sweet fellow! He had a little pair of wings and a bow and arrow! and looked charming.

Besides these grand days we have had Snapdragon, Bullace Pudding, and Apple in Water, as usual. I hope to hear from you soon, and likewise to have some account of your Christmas amusements, as it will amuse me very much when Miss Smith is gone, which I am sorry to say will happen very soon. She goes next Saturday and I assure you I regard it as much more than a disagreeable ceremony, for I hardly know how I shall bear it, she has been so long with us and has been uncommonly kind to me.

The Religion of Plumcake

Robert Southey

Another extract from Letters from England *by the Poet Laureate.*

Just at this time these [pastrycooks'] shops are filled with large plumcakes, which are crusted over with sugar, and ornamented in every possible way. These are for the festival of the kings, it being part of an Englishman's religion to eat plumcake on this day, and to have pies at Christmas made of meat and plums. This is the only way in which these festivals are celebrated; and if the children had not an interest in keeping it up, even this would be soon disused. All persons say how differently this season was observed in their fathers' days, and speak of old ceremonies and old festivities as things which are obsolete. The cause is obvious. In large towns the populace is continually shifting; a new settler neither continues the customs of his own province in a place where they would be strange, nor adopts those which he finds, because they are strange to him, and thus all local differences are wearing out. In the country, estates are purchased by new men, by the manufacturing and merchantile aristocracy who have no family customs to keep up, and by planters from the West Indies, and adventurers from the East who have no feeling connected with times and seasons which they have so long ceased to observe.

A Christmas Baby

Letter from Charles Austen

*Jane's youngest brother Charles John eventually became a sea captain.
He married Frances Palmer and they had four children. After her death
he married again to Harriet Palmer, and they had four more children.
The following letter from Charles to his sister Cassandra, Jane's elder*

sister, written from Bermuda on Christmas Eve 1808, tells the news of the birth of Charles' and Fanny's firstborn, Cassandra Esten. Unfortunately, parts of the letter are almost indecipherable, so there are a few missing words here and there. He refers to the birth not only of his own daughter, but of his wife's sister's son, within a week of each other, and tells Cassandra that he wishes her to be one of the four godparents, presumably by proxy.

My Dear Cassandra,

I am sure that you will be delighted to hear that my beloved Fanny was safely delivered a fine girl on the 22nd of December, and that they are both doing remarkably well. The Baby [. . .] being the first that ever was seen is really a good looking healthy young lady of very large dimensions and as fat as butter. I mean to call her Cassandra Esten and by the favour of you to be a Sponsor your [. . .] will be Mrs Esten and Captain [. . .] Mrs [. . .] your other partner. I esteem myself very fortunate in having been allowed to be in port at this critical moment to support my Fanny, who has been prevented from enjoying her sister's society owing to her having been employed in the same way. She was safely delivered of a little boy just a week before his cousin Cassandra made her entrance into this world contrary to [. . .] he is by far the longest but he is a healthy little fellow and as well as his mother doing very well, which I am sure will give you pleasure tho' you are not personally acquainted with the parties.

I wrote to Jane about a fortnight ago acquainting her with my arrival at this place and of my having captured a little Frenchman which I am very sorry to add has never reached this port and which she has [. . .] to the West Indies. I have lost her and what is a real misfortune the loss of twelve of my people, two of them dead I have had but little hope of ever hearing of her. The weather has been very severe since we captured her. The Admiral and his family arrived just a fortnight ago and [. . .] for the winter, I find them friendly as ever.

I wish you a merry and happy Xmas in which I am [. . .] in sending the love of her Dear Grandmother and Aunt for our little Cassandra. The October and November mails have not yet reached us so that I know nothing about you of late, I hope you have been more fortunate in hearing of me. I expect to sail on Thursday with a small convoy for the Island of Domingo . . .

Skating at Ratzeburg

A short item from The Friend *magazine of 1809, by S.T. Coleridge.*

The lower lake is now all alive with skaters, and by ladies driven onward by them in their ice-cars. Mercury, surely, was the first maker of skates, and the wings at his feet are symbols of the invention. In skating there are three pleasing circumstances: the infinitely subtle particles of ice which the skate cuts up, and which creep and run before the skate like a low mist, and in sunrise or sunset become coloured; second, the shadow of the skater in the water, seen through the transparent ice; and third the melancholy undulating sound from the skate, not without variety; and when very many are skating together, the sounds and the noises give an impulse to the icy trees, and the woods all around the lake tinkle.

Mistletoe: A Charade in Three Acts

An original late eighteenth-century parlour play such as those Jane Austen's family enjoyed.

ACT I.
MISTLE – (Mizzle.)
DRAMATIS PERSONÆ.

POOR TENANT.   HIS WIFE.   HIS FAMILY.

ANGRY LANDLORD.

SCENE – *House of Poor Tenant comfortably furnished.*

Enter POOR TENANT in a state of extreme dejection. HIS WIFE, who follows him, endeavours to console him, but in vain, for he only stamps and presses his forehead the more. She clings to him and demands the cause of his sorrow. He pulls from his pocket a placard written, 'RENT DAY TO-MORROW.' She falls back in horror, and weeps.

Enter HIS FAMILY, who, seeing their Father and Mother's affliction, are overcome by their feelings. They turn aside their heads and sob audibly.

Poor Tenant addresses His Family. He a second time exhibits his placard, and the sorrow of the group becomes extreme. He tells them, by pulling his pockets inside out, that he has not a penny. He points to his comfortable furniture, and informs them that the Angry Landlord will seize it all for rent. Sinking into a chair, he is overwhelmed in his grief. His Wife and Family gather round him, and ask in what way they can assist him. They offer to bear away their goods that night, and carry them beyond the reach of the Angry Landlord. A gleam of joy passes over the countenance of Poor Tenant. He embraces his children, and His Wife blesses them.

His Family then seize the chairs, and carry them on tiptoe into the passage. They return stealthily, until the whole room is stripped. Then casting a long farewell look at the ceiling of their forefathers' home – they strike a touching tableau, and *exeunt* Poor Tenant, His Wife, and Family, mournfully.

Enter, ANGRY LANDLORD, with a pen in his mouth and a ledger under his arm. He stamps loudly on the floor of Poor Tenant's house, but nobody comes. He stamps again and again, his face wearing an expression of surprise and disgust. In a great passion he raves about the room, expressing in action his indignation at all the furniture having been removed. He swears to be revenged, and draws a writ from his pocket.

Exit Angry Landlord, still swearing vengeance.

ACT II.
–TOE
DRAMATIS PERSONÆ.

| THE POPE OF ROME. | CARDINALS. | PRIESTS. |
| IRISH GENTLEMAN. | ENGLISH GENTLEMAN. | PAPAL SOLDIERS. |

SCENE – *Interior of a Chapel at Rome. Around it are hung pictures, and at the end is the arm-chair for the Pope's throne.*

Enter IRISH GENTLEMAN and ENGLISH GENTLEMAN arm-in-arm, to view the beauties of the chapel. They are both delighted with the pictures, and while the Irish Gentleman kneels down, the English one carves his name on the door, to tell all further visitors that he has been there.

The solemn music of a piano is heard, and

Enter THE POPE OF ROME, dressed in full canonicals of red table-cover and lace cuffs. He walks grandly, and is followed by CARDINALS in sacerdotal robes of bed-curtains, and devout PRIESTS in ladies' cloaks with the hoods over their heads. They tell their beads of coral necklaces.

The Pope seats himself in the arm-chair throne, and the Priests commence kissing his toe. He blesses each one as he rises. The Irish Gentleman advancing, beseeches by gestures Cardinals to allow him to take one fond embrace. They are pleased with his earnestness, and consent. He casts himself on his knees and kisses it madly.

They then invite the English Gentleman also to advance and be blessed. He folds his arms and refuses disdainfully. The Pope is enraged, and rises from his throne. The Cardinals gather menacingly round English Gentleman, and the Priests threaten him with wild gesticulations. The Irish Gentleman in vain endeavours to restore peace. His friend is once more besought to yield, but still refuses. The Pope beckons to his priests, when

Enter PAPAL SOLDIERS, and surround English Gentleman, who still remains with his arms crossed. He refuses to stir, and addresses the Pope and his Court in language of contempt. The Guards are ordered to do their duty, and force English Gentleman away with the point of their brooms. (*Soft Music.*)

Exeunt Pope, Cardinals, and Priests, solemnly, the Irish Gentleman cheering.

ACT III.

MISTLETOE

DRAMATIS PERSONÆ.

GRANDFATHER.   HIS SON.

GRANDMOTHER.   HER DAUGHTER (*Wife to His Son*).

THEIR CHILDREN.   VISITORS.   SERVANTS.   MUSICIANS.

SCENE – *Old Hall in the Mansion of His Son. Long table down the centre, with chairs.*

Enter SERVANTS bearing grand feast, which they arrange on the table. They then stand behind the chairs.

Enter GRANDFATHER, GRANDMOTHER, HIS SON, HER DAUGHTER, THEIR CHILDREN, and VISITORS in holiday costume. Grandfather is so old he can scarcely walk, and is supported by His Son, whom he blesses. Grandmother is placed next to Her Daughter, and Their Children dance about with delight. When they are seated at table, they eat.

Enter Servants bearing large dish with brown silk bundle in it for plum-pudding. Their Children rise from the table and dance round it.

As soon as the dinner is removed, His Son gives a signal, when

Enter MUSICIANS with imitation instruments in their hands. Their Children serve them with wine and plum-pudding. (*Affecting picture.*) Grandfather goes out and fetches a bunch of Mistletoe, which he hangs to the lamp. They all laugh, and are delighted with the wickedness of Grandfather. He laughs and coughs a great deal, and all Their Children thump him on the back to make him better.

The Visitors then take the Young Ladies, who appear dreadfully bashful, and drag them screaming and tittering under the Mistletoe, where they embrace them theatrically, by crossing their heads over their shoulders.

Grandmother is delighted, and presses her sides with mirth, when one of Their Children takes her hand, and pulls her under the Mistletoe and kisses her. Grandfather pretends to be jealous, and the fun increases.

Several of the Gentlemen are smitten with the charms of the Ladies, and after they have kissed them, proceed to the corners, where they fall on one knee and propose. The Ladies weep, hesitate, and point to Grandfather. The Gentlemen beseech the Grandfather to consent. He weeps, and blesses them.

Musicians begin playing a court dance, all the party standing up. The old Grandfather taking Grandmother's hand, leads off the dance.

Strong Beer and a Parcel from London

Revd William Holland

More of the Revd Holland's seasonal diary jottings, this time from 1807.

Friday 25 December 1807
Christmas Day, a pleasant gentle thaugh. We had not so many at Church as I expected and fewer than I remember at the Sacrament. They were all women except Mr Thomas Rich, the Clerk and I being the necessary and Official Attendants at the Communion Table. I found not many at Dodington. We had twelve people to dine in the kitchen where they had Port, Beef and Plum Pudding and as good strong beer after dinner as ever was drunk. The Clerk of Dodington who dined here I presented with a good old black coat of mine, of which he stood in need for he is but a miserable wight and drinks up every thing and keeps himself as poor as a Church Mouse. He is so bad a stick that he is obliged to have his old mother look out the lessons.

Saturday 26 December 1807
George has been permitted to go with his father to visit his friends. I charged him to come home in good time but he has not made his

'We had twelve people to dine . . .'

appearance and it is past nine. Wm Frost had his son-in-law, wife and children come and see him this Christmastime and has a son-in-law wife and child besides in the house so that I cannot conceive where he can put them all yet it is pleasant to see families meet on Christmas.

Thursday 31 December 1807

A parcel from London from Mrs Dodwell. Silk for a gown for my wife and a very handsome Court Calendar bound in Morocco, a present for me. Indeed it has in it twice what others have in general with the Peerage of England and Baronets and their respective incomes and supporters and various other articles. It has clasps and is as thick as a small bible, in short a very capital present.

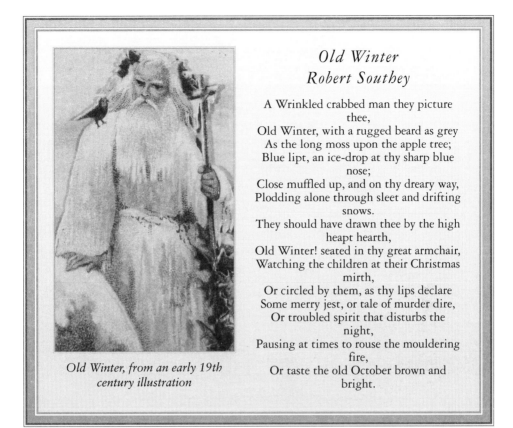

Old Winter
Robert Southey

A Wrinkled crabbed man they picture
thee,
Old Winter, with a rugged beard as grey
As the long moss upon the apple tree;
Blue lipt, an ice-drop at thy sharp blue
nose;
Close muffled up, and on thy dreary way,
Plodding alone through sleet and drifting
snows.
They should have drawn thee by the high
heapt hearth,
Old Winter! seated in thy great armchair,
Watching the children at their Christmas
mirth,
Or circled by them, as thy lips declare
Some merry jest, or tale of murder dire,
Or troubled spirit that disturbs the
night,
Pausing at times to rouse the mouldering
fire,
Or taste the old October brown and
bright.

*Old Winter, from an early 19th
century illustration*

Christmas at Godmersham Park, 1808–9

Fanny Austen writes to Miss Chapman on Christmas Day 1808

The boys are all very happy at the thought of seeing you again, they came home the 16th and will most likely return to school at the end of January. By the by, as I am writing on Xmas Day, it is proper to wish you a merry Xmas and a happy new year, which I do with all my heart. Our amusements began yesterday, when Miss Medwin and all the Morris's (Sophia being now at home) drank tea with us, and in the

A coach and horses in the snow

evening we had (to us), a delightful ball (though of course beneath your notice) which began at 7 and ended at 10. We had twelve dances and sometimes 5, 6 or 7 couples at different times. I danced nine and played three – we then had a game of Hunt the Slipper and ended the day with sandwiches and tarts. I must not omit to say that the little ones dressed up as usual and sang Christmas Carols.

Fanny then goes on to describe Christmas Day, and the gifts and the 'Christmas Boxes' (containing money) which were given to the children in the party, Fanny herself receiving two whole guineas (£2.10). She tells of the children's visit to the servants' hall to sing carols there, and the excited anticipation with which they looked forward to being allowed to join the grown-ups for the grand Christmas dinner party at the fashionable eating hour of four o'clock. The servants joined the party to toast the season, and the children sang yet more carols, this time collecting money to distribute to the poor.

On the Eve of Twelfth Night the company collected together for several little dances to Aunt L's playing, and before she came I was the performer and of course did not get much dancing before Blind John, who used to play the Harp at the servants' Balls, was called in and played twelve dances for the gathered company.

from

The Sketch Book of Geoffrey Crayon

Washington Irving

In his Sketch Book *Washington Irving (1783–1859) noted many elements of British social life and culture, written as an American travelling through Britain. The* Sketch Book *became as great a favourite in England as it was later to become in America. The Christmas notes are so accurate that it has become one of our greatest reference works for the study of the Georgian Christmas. The following extracts are taken from the original edition of 1819.*

Of the Spirit of Christmas 1810

The world has become more worldly. There is more of dissipation, and less of enjoyment. Pleasure has expanded into a broader but shallower stream; and has forsaken many of those deep and quiet channels where it flowed sweetly through the calm bosom of domestic life. Society has acquired a more enlightened and elegant tone, but it has lost many of its peculiarities, its home-bred feelings, its honest fireside delights. The traditional customs of golden hearted antiquity. Its feudal hospitalities and lordly wassailings have passed away with the baronial castles and the stately manor-houses in which they were celebrated. They comported with the shadowy hall, the great oaken gallery and the tapestried parlour, but are unfitted in the light showy saloons and gay drawing rooms of the modern villa.

Shorn however, as it is, of its ancient and festive honours, Christmas is still a period of delightful excitement in England. It is gratifying to see that home feeling completely aroused which holds so powerful a place in every English bosom. The preparations making on every side for the social board that is again to unite friends and kindred; the presents of good cheer passing and repassing, those tokens of regard, and quickeners of kind feelings; the evergreens distributed about houses and churches, emblems of peace and gladness: all these have the most pleasing effect in producing fond associations, and kindling benevolent sympathies. Even the sound of the Waits, rude as may be their minstrelsy, breaks up the midwatch of a winter's night with the effect of perfect harmony. As I have been awakened by them in that still and solemn hour, 'when deep sleep falleth upon man', I have listened with a hushed delight, and connecting them with the sacred and joyous occasion, have almost fancied them into another celestial choir, announcing peace and goodwill to mankind.

Christmas at Bracebridge Hall

Geoffrey Crayon is travelling through Yorkshire on Christmas Eve . . .

In the course of a December tour in Yorkshire, I rode for a long distance in one of the public coaches, on the day preceding Christmas. The coach was crowded, both inside and out, with passengers who, by their talk, seemed principally bound to the mansions of relations or friends, to eat Christmas dinner. It was loaded also with hampers of game, and baskets and boxes of delicacies; and hares hung dangling their long ears about the coachman's box, presents from distant friends for the impending feast.

I had three rosy-cheeked boys for my fellow passengers inside, full of the buxom health which I have observed in the children of this country. They were returning home for the holidays in high glee, and promising themselves a world of enjoyment. It was delightful to hear the gigantic plans of the little rogues . . .

They were under the particular guardianship of the coachman, to whom, whenever an opportunity presented itself, they addressed a host of questions, and pronounced him one of the best fellows in the world. Indeed

I could not but notice the more than ordinary air of bustle and importance of the coachman, who wore his hat on one side, and had a large bunch of Christmas greens stuck in the buttonhole of his coat. He is always a personage full of mighty care and business, but he is particularly so this season having so many commissions to execute in consequence of the great inter-change of presents. And here, perhaps, it may not be unaccept-able to my untravelled readers to have a sketch that may serve as a general representation of this very numerous and important class of functionaries, who have a dress, a manner, a language, and air peculiar to themselves and prev-alent throughout the fraternity, so

'. . . Whenever an English stage Coachman is seen, he cannot be mistaken for one of any other craft . . .', The Stagecoach, Washington Irving

that wherever an English stage coachman may be seen he cannot be mistaken for one of any other craft or mystery.

He had commonly, a broad, full face, curiously mottled with red, as if the blood has been forced by hard feeding into every vessel of the skin; he is swelled into jolly dimensions by frequent potations of malt liquors, and his bulk is still further increased by a multiplicity of coats in which he is buried like a cauliflower . . . He wears a broadbrimmed low crowned hat, a huge roll of coloured handkerchief around his neck . . . His waistcoat is commonly of some bright colour, and his small clothes extend far below the knees to meet with a pair of jockey boots . . .

A stagecoach carries animation along with it . . . The horn, sounded at the entrance to a village, produces a general bustle. Some hasten forth to meet friends, some with bundles and bandboxes to secure places, and in the hurry of the moment can hardly take leave of the group that accompanies them. In the meantime the coachman has a world of small commissions to exercise . . .

'. . . The kitchen of an English Inn . . . hung round with copper and tin utensils and decorated with Christmas Greens . . .'

Perhaps the impending holiday might have given a more than usual animation to the country . . . Game, poultry, and other luxuries for the table, were in brisk circulation in the villages; the grocers' butchers' and fruiterers' shops were thronged with customers. The housewives were stirring briskly about putting their dwellings in order; and the glossy branches of holly, with their bright red berries, began to appear at the windows . . .

In the evening we reached a village where I was determined to pass the night. As we drove into the great gateway of the Inn, I saw on one side the light of a rousing kitchen fire beaming through a window. I entered, and admired for the hundredth time, that picture of convenience, neatness, and broad honest enjoyment, the kitchen of an English Inn. It was of spacious dimensions, hung round with copper and tin vessels highly polished, and decorated here and there with a Christmas green. Hams, tongues and flitches of bacon were suspended from the ceiling; a smoke jack made its ceaseless clanking beside the fireplace, and a clock ticked in one corner. A well-scoured deal table extended along one side of the kitchen, with a cold round of beef and other viands upon it, over which two foaming tankards of ale seemed mounting guard. Travellers of inferior order were preparing to attack this stout repast, while others sat smoking and gossiping over their ale on two high back oaken settles beside the fire . . .

I had not been long at the inn when a post-chaise drove up to the door. A young gentleman stepped out . . . whose countenance which I thought I knew . . . It was Frank Bracebridge, a sprightly, good humoured fellow with whom I had once travelled on the Continent . . . Finding that I was not pressed for time . . . he insisted that I should give him a day or two at his father's country seat . . . 'It is better than eating a solitary Christmas dinner at an inn,' said he, 'and I can assure you of a hearty welcome in something of the old fashioned style' . . . I closed therefore at once, with his invitation; the chaise drove to the door, and in a few moments I was on my way to the family mansion of the Bracebridges . . .

Geoffrey Crayon gives account of his first impressions of the stately pile, the sounds and sight and smells of a traditional Yorkshire Christmas Eve filling his senses . . .

It was a brilliant moonlight night, but extremely cold; the chaise whirled rapidly over the frozen ground . . .

As we approached the house, we heard the sound of music, and now and then a burst of laughter, from one end of the building. This, Bracebridge said, must proceed from the servants' hall, where a great deal of revelry was permitted, and even encouraged by the squire, throughout the twelve days of Christmas, provided everything was done conformably to ancient usage. Here were kept up the old games of Hoodman Blind, shoe the wild mare, hot cockles, steal the white loaf, bob apple, and snap dragon; the Yule clog and Christmas candle were regularly burnt, and the mistletoe with its white berries, hung up, to the imminent peril of all the pretty housemaids . . .

Supper was announced shortly after our arrival. It was served up in a

The dancers young and old, by Randolph Caldicott

spacious oaken chamber, the panels of which shone with wax and around which were several family portraits decorated with Holly and Ivy. Besides the accustomed lights, two great wax tapers, called Christmas candles, wreathed with greens, were placed on a high polished buffet among the family plate. The table was abundantly spread with substantial fare; but the squire made his supper of frumenty, a dish made of wheat cakes boiled in milk, with rich spices . . .

I was happy to find my old friend Minc'd Pie in the retinue of the feast; and finding him to be perfectly orthodox, and that I need not be ashamed of my predilection, I greeted him with all the warmth wherewith we usually greet an old and very genteel acquaintance . . .

The supper had disposed everyone to gaiety, and an old harper was summoned from the servants' hall . . . The dance, like most dances after supper, was a merry one; some of the older folk joined in it, and the squire himself figured down several couple with a partner, with who he affirmed he had danced every Christmas for nearly half a century. Master Simon, who seemed to be a connecting link between the old times and the new, and to be withal a little antiquated with the tastes of his accomplishments, evidently piqued himself on his dancing and was attempting to gain credit by the heel toe rigadoon, and other graces of the ancient school; but he had unluckily assorted himself with a little romping girl from boarding school, who, by her wild vivacity, kept him continually on the stretch and defeated all his sober attempts at elegance . . .

The young Oxonian, on the contrary, had led out one of his maiden aunts, on whom the rogue played a thousand little knaveries with impunity: he was full of practical jokes and his delight was to tease his aunts and cousins . . . the most interesting couple in the dance was the young officer and a ward of the squires, a beautiful, blushing girl of seventeen. From several shy glances which I had noticed in the course of the evening, I suspected there was a little kindness growing up between them; and indeed, the young soldier was just the hero to captivate a romantic girl. He was tall, slender and handsome, and, like most of the young British officers of late years, had picked up various small accomplishments on the Continent: he could talk French and Italian, draw landscapes, sing very tolerably, dance divinely; but above all, he had been wounded at Waterloo: what girl of seventeen well read in poetry and romance, could resist such a mirror of chivalry and perfection! . . .

The party now broke up for the night with the kindhearted old custom of shaking hands. As I passed through the hall on the way to my chamber, the dying embers of the Yule log still sent forth a dusky glow, and had it not been 'the season when no spirit dares stir abroad', I should have been half tempted to steal from my room at midnight, and peep whether the fairies might not be at their revels about the hearth.

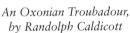

*An Oxonian Troubadour,
by Randolph Caldicott*

My chamber was in the old part of the mansion . . . I had scarcely got into bed when a strain of music seemed to break forth in the air just below the window. I listened, and found it proceeded from a band, which I concluded to be the Waits from some neighbouring village. They went round the house playing under the windows. I drew aside the curtains to hear them more distinctly. The sounds as they receded, became more soft and aerial, and seemed to accord with the quiet and the moonlight. I listened and listened; they became more and more tender and remote, and, as they gradually died away, my head sunk upon the pillow, and I fell asleep.

Geoffrey goes on to describe waking up on Christmas morning to the tradition of the children of the household singing 'Christians Awake' at the doors of all the guests' rooms . . .

When I awoke the next morning, it seemed as if all the events of the preceding evening had been a dream, and nothing but the identity of the ancient chamber in which I lay convinced me of their reality . . . While I lay

Christmas Day Revellers, by Randolph Caldicott

musing on my pillows I heard the sound of little feet pattering outside of the door, and a whispering consultation. Presently a choir of small voices chanted forth an old Christmas carol, the burdon of which was,

> Rejoice our Saviour he was born
> On Christmas day in the morning.

I rose softly, slipped on my clothes, opened the door suddenly, and beheld one of the most beautiful little fairy groups that a painter could imagine. It consisted of a boy and two girls, the eldest not more than six, and lovely as seraphs. They were going the rounds of the house, and singing at every chamber door; but my sudden appearance frightened them into mute bashfulness. They remained for a moment playing on their lips with their fingers, and now and then stealing a shy glance from under their eyebrows, until, as if by one impulse, they scampered away, and as they turned on the angle of the gallery, I heard them laughing in triumph at their escape.

The account goes on at length to describe breakfast, the staff, the trip to church and even the sermon: Irving was nothing if not thorough! The next extract finds the family back at Bracebridge Hall after the service, with a description of the villagers coming for their traditional Christmas dole.

A few years before he had kept open house during the holidays in the old style. The country people, however, did not understand how to play their parts in the scene of hospitality; many uncouth circumstances occurred; the manor was overrun by all the vagrants of the country, and more beggars drawn into the neighbourhood in one week than the parish officers could get rid of in a year. Since then, he had contented himself with inviting the decent part of the neighbouring

*'Three children heralding in Christmas morn',
by Randolph Caldicott*

Coach Miseries

A gentleman writes to Notes and Queries *in 1856 to recall 'two coach miseries' that regularly occurred on his Christmas homecomings from school when he was a child.*

Arriving at daybreak, more than half famished, after an excessively cold winter's night riding on the box, with fingers too benumbed to assist you in the partaking of the solids at the breakfast table, and receiving the summons of – 'Now, Gentlemen! Coach is waiting!' just as the prospect of returning circulation gives you hope of getting a meal.

Prepared against the 'pelting of the pitiless storm', with wraps and waterproofs, cape and apron etc. to find that, from a point of your female neighbour's umbrella, which continually tickles your ear, and threatens to upset your hat, a regular stream is conducted down your neck, common politeness forbidding you to remonstrate.

peasantry to call at the hall on Christmas day, and with distributing beef, and bread, and ale, among the poor, that they might make merry in their own dwellings.

We had not been long home when the sound of music was heard from a distance. A band of country lads, without coats, their shirt sleeves fancifully tied with ribbons, their hats decorated with greens, and clubs in their hands, were seen advancing up the avenue, followed by a large number of villagers and peasantry. They stopped before the hall door, where the music struck up a peculiar air, and the lads performed a curious and intricate dance, advancing, retreating and striking their clubs together, keeping exact time to the music; while one, whimsically crowned with a fox's skin, the tail of which flaunted down his back, kept capering round the skirts of the dance, and rattling a Christmas box with many antic gesticulations.

Winter Balls and Festive Soups

Imagine putting on a fine ballgown, décolleté, floaty and clinging, leaving no room for flannel petticoats, your hair dressed in such a way that only the flimsiest scarf can protect your head from the cold night. The coach offers little protection, draughty. What you need when you arrive at the Christmas Ball is a bowl of soup to put colour in the cheeks before greeting the other guests and old acquaintances there, already glowing from their own partaking of the soup, the wine and the dancing. Such would have been the experience of Jane and her characters at every winter ball they attended. She tells us in her novels that such a soup, fortified with 'negus' – a mixture of hot water mixed with sweet wine and lemon, and strongly spiced and poured onto the soup as it was served – was considered a necessity on these occasions.
In Mansfield Park *Jane tells of Fanny's weary but happy escape from the dancing.*

Creeping slowly up the principal staircase, pursued by the ceaseless country-dance, feverish with hopes and fears, soup and negus, sore-footed and fatigued, restless and agitated, yet feeling, in spite of everything, that a Ball was indeed delightful.

A particularly warming soup of the day, written down by Martha Lloyd in her famous leather-bound receipt book, is Cowheel Soup:

Make a strong gravy with shin of beef, a pr. of cow heels boiled tender, then cut them in pieces and take out the bones. One hour before dinner season the gravy with marjoram, savoury thyme, the green of onions, parsley, 1 shalot, chp't fine – of each a teaspoon. Half a pint of Madeira or Sherry, four large spoonfuls of walnut and two of mushroom catchup, pepper, and salt to your taste. Flour the feet and put them in the stewpan with the gravy and just before it is sent to the table, add to a little of the soup almost cold, the yolks of two eggs and a little flour. Beat well together in a saucepan then boil it up. Put it to the soup and then give it all one boil up.

Served without the final flourish of the meat and eggs, this could well have been served at any ball. A more elegant soup to serve at the best parties, which was served at the great Georgian houseparties at Tredegar House in Monmouthshire, was Hartshorn Jelly. This soup was often served in crystal glasses, and the hartshorn was said to have an aphrodisiac effect. Martha's recipe is as follows:

To 4 oz of Hartshorn shavings, one quart of water and boil it dry then put another quart of water and boil it till it will jelly, the whites of two eggs and beat them to a froth with the juice of one lemon and half an orange, a stick of cinnamon and sugar to your taste, run your jelly through a bag and let it stand to be a little cool before you put your eggs to it. Then boil it till it looks clear, or the eggs begin to sink, then run it through the bag until it is quite clear.

Tredegar House's recipe is much the same and adds mulled madeira or sherry at the last minute. As hartshorn is an impossible ingredient to find, I have had success by substituting pigs' trotters!

More Balls and Fashions

Jane's writings are full of descriptions of balls and fashions: dancing was obviously her great love – next to reading and writing that is! Here are some extracts from a few of the Christmas and winter season letters she wrote to her sisters and cousins.

Steventon, Saturday 9 January 1796

My dear Cassandra,

In the first place I hope you will live twenty-three years longer. Mr Tom Lefroy's birthday was yesterday so you are very near of an age.

After this necessary preamble I shall proceed to inform you that we had an exceeding good ball last night . . . We were so terribly good as to take James in our carriage, though there were three of us before, but indeed he deserves encouragement for the very great improvement which has taken place lately in his dancing. Miss Heathcote is pretty, but not near so handsome as I expected. Mr H. began with Elizabeth and afterwards danced with her again; but they do not know how to be particular. I flatter myself however that they will profit by the three successive lessons which I have given them. You scold me so much in the nice long letter which I have in this moment received from you, that I am almost afraid to tell you how my Irish friend and I behaved. Imagine to yourself everything most profligate and shocking in the way of dancing, and sitting down together. I can expose myself, however, only once more, because he leaves the country soon after next Friday, on which day we are to have a dance at Ashe after all. He is a very gentlemanlike, goodlooking, pleasant young man, I assure you. But as to our ever having met, except at the last three balls, I cannot say much; for he is so excessively laughed at about me at Ashe, that he is ashamed of coming to Steventon and ran away when we called on Mrs Lefroy a few days ago . . . Everybody is extremely anxious for your return, but as you cannot come home by the Ashe Ball, I am glad that I have not fed them with false hopes. James danced with Althea, and cut up the turkey last night with great perseverance.

Early January 1808

. . . A large circle of acquaintance and an increase of amusement is quite in character with our approaching removal. Yes – I mean to go to as many balls as possible, that I may have a good bargain. Everybody is very much concerned at our going away, and everybody is acquainted with Chawton and speaks of it as a remarkably pretty village . . . I am very much obliged to Mrs Knight for such a proof of the interest she takes in me, and she may depend upon it that I will marry Mr Papillon, whatever may be his reluctance or my own. I owe her much more than such a trifling sacrifice. Our Ball was rather more amusing than I expected, Martha liked it very much, and I did not gape till the last quarter of an hour. It was past nine before we were sent for, and not twelve when we returned. The room was tolerably full, and there were perhaps thirty couples of dancers. The melancholy part was to see so many dozen young women standing without partners, and each of them with two ugly naked shoulders!

It was the same room in which we danced fifteen years ago! I thought it over, and in spite of the shame of being so much older, felt with thankfulness that I was quite as happy now as then. We paid an additional shilling for our tea, which we took as we chose in a very comfortable adjoining room. There were only four dances, and it went to my heart that the Miss Lances should have partners only for two. You will not expect to hear that I was asked to dance but I was – by the gentleman whom we met that Sunday with Captain d'Auverne. We have always kept up a bowing acquaintance since, and being pleased with his black eyes, I spoke to him at the ball, which brought on me this civility. I do not know his name, and he seems so little at home with the English language, that I believe his black eyes may be the best of him . . . I am glad you have Henry with you again; with him and the boys you cannot but have a cheerful, and at times even, a merry Christmas.

The Mistletoe Bough

Thomas Bayly

A gothic legend in rhyme by Thomas Bayly (1797–1839). The story, as with many old folk tales of the oral tradition, has many alterations and additions. It was originally supposed to be an Italian tale, but it became associated with the Lovell family, among others, and has been claimed by more than one county, including the Austen seats of Kent and Hampshire. In the early nineteenth century it was popular as a ghostly and romantic Christmas tale.

The mistletoe hung from the castle walls,
The holly bough hung in the old oak hall
And the Baron's retainers were blithe and gay,
All keeping their Christmas holiday;

The Baron beheld with a father's pride
His beautiful child, young Lovell's bride,
Whilst she, with her bright eyes seemed to be
The star of that goodly company.

'I'm tired of dancing, my love,' she cried,
'Here tarry a moment for me to hide.
And Lovell, be sure thou art first to trace
The clue to my secret hiding place.'

Away she ran and her friends began
Each tower to search, each vault to scan;
And young Lovell cried, 'Oh, where dost thou hide?
I long to find you, my own dear bride.'

They searched all that night, and they searched the next day,
They sought her in vain till a week pass'd away;
In the highest, the lowest, the loneliest spot,
Young Lovell sought wildly, and found her not;

And the years flew by and their grief at last
Was sung as a sorrowing tale of the past,
And when Lovell appeared, the children they cri'd
'See, the old man still weeps for his own dear bride.'

One day an old chest that had long lain hid
Was found in the castle – they rais'd the lid
And a skeletal form lay a-mould'ring there
In the bridal wreath of a lady fair;

O, sad was her fate, in a Yuletide jest,
She hid from her Lord in an old oak chest.
It closed with a spring – what a dreadful doom
The bride lay clasped in an oaken tomb.

Christmas Gambling

Card games play a large part in Christmas celebrations and festivities. Here is a brief comment by that observer of English custom, Robert Southey.

Gambling, dancing and hunting are as favourite pastimes among the English as among savages. The latter of these sports must be almost exclusively the amusement of men; dancing requires youth, or at least strength and agility; but old and young, hale and infirm can alike enjoy the stimulus of the dicebox or the card table . . .

Ombre, Basset, and Quadrille had their day; but Whist is as much the favourite now as when it was first introduced [around 1730]. The more rigid dissenters, and especially the Quakers, proscribe cards altogether; some of the old church-people, on the contrary, seem to ascribe a sort of sacredness to this method of amusement, and think that a Christmas-day cannot be duly celebrated without it. But a general and unaccountable prejudice prevails against the use of them on Sundays. I believe that half the people of England think it the very essence of sabbath-breaking.

Christmas at Godmersham Park, 1811–12

In February 1812, Fanny Austen wrote to her friend Miss Dorothy Clapman with the details of the holiday season that year. Unfortunately, the page is double written, both across and down, making it almost illegible; despite the difficulties in deciphering, it gives such a vivid account of Georgian Christmas festivities that as much of it as possible is reproduced here.

The boys arrived home for Christmas on the coach, and in the pouring rain, which left them with bad colds all through the holiday. It is possible that the 'whooping cough' she refers to was in fact croup, which was common after a rain-soaked cold, and commonly called whooping cough up to the 1940s. It is interesting that while she says that Edward was 'always the delicate one', he in fact outlived Henry and George by many years and died at the age of eighty-five!

The boys enjoyed their holiday very much of course, George and Henry quite lost their coughs, but Edward's continued very uncomfortable till he returned which I did not so much wonder at as he is much more delicate than the others, he writes that he is better since he went back to school. They left us the 30th and I was very sorry to lose them, as you may suppose. The prospect of the Easter holiday being so near, in some measure softens the parting which at times is detestable.

I don't know whether I told you that the Miss Morris's are at home for the Christmas holidays, they are very nice girls and have contributed a good deal to our entertainment.

None of us caught the whooping cough and have been very well the whole time. We have in general had cards, snapdragons, Bullet pudding, etc. on any particular evening, and Whist, Commerce and others and Tickets were the favourite games. I think when cards failed the boys played every evening at Drafts, Chess and Backgammon. On Twelfth night we had a delightful evening though not so grand as last year. Julia, Sophia, W and A dined and spent the evening with us. Uncle and Aunt H B Jane and Mary were here at the same time; about our dress King and Queen, W Morris was King, I was Queen, Papa – Prince Busty Trusty, Mama – Red Riding Hood, Edward – Paddy O'Flaherty, G. – Johnny Bo-peep, H. – Timothy Trip, W. – Moses Abrahams, Eliz. – Mrs O'Flaherty, Ma. – Granny Grump, C [?] – Cupid (by his own desire), Louisa – Princess Busty Trusty, Uncle H.B. – Punch, Aunt H.B. – Poll Mendicant, Jane – Punch's Wife, Mary – Columbine, Uncle John – Jerry the Milkman, Mrs Morris – Sukey Sweetlips, Sophia – Margery Muttonpie.

Soon after, according to a preconsented plan, some of us retired upstairs to dress Jane as Punch's wife, in a witches hat, a green petticoat and scarlet shawl (the remains of our last year's masquerade) Mrs M.J. and I in beggars clothes to sing carols at the parlour door, and myself in a long scarlet cloak for a royal robe and a wreath of natural primroses (which we had gathered and made up in the morning for whoever should be queen) around my head. We then played at Oranges and Lemons, Hunt the Slipper, Wind the Jack . . . we had a very pleasant Ball till 10, sometimes Mama sometimes myself acting as musicians. Jan. 10th was Julia's birthday, and we had another very delightful dance, she was 15 that day, and is rather clever I think. She is not very pretty, but has dark eyes and light hair and a bad shaped face, an awkward figure but a good neck, and rather short for her age. Sophia who was 15 on the 3rd this month, is remarkably short and little for her age but a very pretty figure and dark blue eyes with long lashes and pretty brown hair, I think will be a very pretty woman indeed, she is a great favourite of mine in person and disposition and though not so animated as her sisters, is a very sweet girl. I am much obliged to you for your good wishes on my birthday.

Emma's Christmas Presents

❧

Emma Austen Leigh, a niece of Jane, kept a record of all her gifts from 1813 to 1821. This 'gift diary' gives a wonderful insight into the sort of presents exchanged in the later Georgian and Regency period.

1813
Papa – A Tambourine
Mamma – A Compass Case
Miss Ramsey – A straw box, empty
Aunt – A Parallel ruler

1815
Mamma – A mariner's compass
Aunt – A silver vinagrette
Augusta – A gold twisted ring
Miss Ramsey – A leather purse

1816
Mamma – A gold chain
Aunt – A coral broach
Miss Ramsey – A nitting box her own drawing on the top
Augusta – China candlestick
Fanny – A silk box. The winders made by her

1817
Mamma – A pair of gold earrings
Fanny – A turquoise ring
Aunt – A gold locket with her hair
Miss Ramsey – A green silk and silver purse, her own making

1818 By the tree

Mamma – A Thermometer

Aunt – An Amethyst cross

Augusta – A cut glass standing smelling casket

Fanny – A card nitting box, drawn on the top and made by her

Eliza – A needlecase and pincushion, her own making

Charlotte – A work bag, ditto.

Drummond – A broach

Maria – An Anchor pin

Miss Ramsey – A worked trimming of her own making

Belinda Colebrooke – A silk workbox, butterflies on the top

Harriot Colebrooke – A pink and white cornelian cross

1819

Mamma – A fur Tippet

Aunt – A Belgian leather workbox

Charles – A rosebud Broach

Eliza – A Peacock feather screen, her own making

Charlotte – A pair of Ruffles, ditto.

Drummond – A memorandum book, ditto.

Maria – A pincushion, ditto.

1820

Mamma – A pr of long gold earrings

Aunt – A coral necklace

Fanny – A silver vinagrette

Charlotte – A red leather inkstand box

Maria – A little ring

Early nineteenth-century gifts, by
Frances Vallaydon-Pillay

1821

Aunt – A rosewood jewel box

Augusta – An ivory opera glass

Fanny – A blue bead necklace, she strung

Eliza – A penknife

Charlotte – A white satin pincushion

Belinda and Harriot – A splendid hair bracelet and clasp, their own hair

Charles brought me from abroad
A blue, gold and silver turban
Genoa and French flowers
Lyons lavender coloured silk gown
Belgian silk scarf
French worked muslin handkerchief
Steel buckle
Cut coral necklace and earrings and coral cameo ring and coral head fringes
Vienna enamel cross and fastenings
Moscow turquoise set in a ring at Vienna
Vienna mother of pearl trunk
Tartarian or chinese scent bag
Biscuit figure of a good girl from Dresden
Quantity of Petis Gris, or squirrel furs
Silver chains and dangler
Music

Christmas at Tredegar House

Tredegar House, on the Welsh/English border in South Wales, was the seat of the great Morgan family. During the time of Jane Austen, the family enlarged and modernized their home extensively, so that the major part of the house, which is now open to the public, is essentially Austen period. Because of this, many Austen aficionados have visited, dreaming of the great balls and houseparties described in Jane Austen's novels, and have even been able to colour their dreams by seeing Austen exhibitions and lecture tours.
The following is an extract from the Shrewsbury Chronicle *in 1813.*

According to an annual custom, the mansion of Sir Charles Morgan, Baronet, was thrown open at Christmas and the usual hospitality reigned until the 10th inst. [of January] Upwards of sixty persons of the first distinction had accommodation in the house and, it being the rule of the house never to suffer either servant or horse to depart, so long as room can be found, they also were entertained.

A better masquerade was never witnessed . . . At two o'clock supper was announced, when a greater display of beauty in fancy dresses of unrivalled taste and elegance, never appeared; and the profusion of diamonds and pearls added much to the splendour of the scene. Soon after supper the merry dance commenced, and was kept up with spirit until a late hour . . . Tredegar was one continued scene of mirth, good humour and jocularity. Champagne, Burgundy, white and red Hermitage, and every expensive wine were served with the utmost profusion.

Among the papers at Tredegar House is a scribbled rhyme, written, one assumes, by a member of the family or even of the upper domestic household, after the Twelfth Night party in 1812.

> Tredegar concluded with a Grand Masquerade.
> Some of the party in grief and deep sorrow
> Ordered the chaises and off on the morrow.
> Capt. Ellis and wife for Abergavenny,
> Having, as gypsies, told the fortunes of many.
> Mr Price and his Lady to Llanwern were to dine
> Miss Davis obliged the party to join.
> Slaughters and Richardson went the next day
> Hearts were so heavy not a word could they say.
> Oh! Had you but seen the Kirby's in grief
> And several young beaux offering relief.
> Miss Molyneux next alas! The poor creatures,
> How cruelly grief distorted their features;
> The decorous ladies before they departed
> Declared one and all they were all broken hearted.
> Treharris and Miss Richards from Lochtraheen
> So burdened with tears not fit to be seen.

*This extract from the memoirs of General Sir Thomas Molyneux
describes one family's impression of Charles Morgan's famed Christmas
hospitality.*

In December 1808, we went to spend the Christmas with Sir Charles Morgan at Tredegar in Monmouthshire for the first time. There was an immense large party there consisting of Gentlemen and Ladies, as many servants who were entertained in the Servants Hall, and above 100 horses in this hospitable baronet's stables.

We continued to pay our annual visits to him every Christmas for the ensuing eight years, generally went there 28th December, the day after my birthday (not wishing to be from home on that, or on Christmas Day), and remained till about 10th January at which time the party generally dispersed.

Twelfth Night Festivities

In Georgian England, much of the 'gaieties' of Christmas seemed to revolve around Twelfth Night, the last eve of Christmas, and Feast of the Epiphany, or visit of the Wise Men. By 1870, this custom had been officially stopped as a result of Queen Victoria objecting to the riotousness of the occasion, thus it is the one Christmas tradition which was quelled by the Victorians rather than enhanced.

In Georgian England, however, it heralded the end of the Christmas season, and was the time for the solemnity of the religious observance to cease, for the guests to go home, for decorations to be taken down. This was effected usually by a grand fancy ball, a masque or fancy dress, either on Twelve Night itself or within a few days, depending on other big social events in the area. Sometimes these balls were called the Grand Christmas Ball, the Children's Ball or Family Ball, and included invitations for the children of the invitees. One such party is referred to by Jane in her letter to Cassandra of 27 December 1808:

I was happy to hear, chiefly for Anne's sake, that a ball at Manydown was once more in agitation; it is called a child's ball, and given by Mrs Heathcote to Wm. Such was its beginning at least, but it will probably swell into something more. Edward was invited during his stay at Manydown, and it is to take place between this and Twelfth-day. Mrs Hulbert has taken Anne a pair of white shoes on the occasion.

The diary of the country parson William Holland, which he kept from 1799 to 1818, gives another account (Friday 29 December 1815):

In the afternoon we had a famous ball where children were admitted, the Christmas Ball. My wife and I and two children went with Mr and Mrs Edward Sealy. It was indeed a very good Ball. There my wife and I saw our children both dance at the same time and they made a good figure. It was very late before we returned and our young ones staid behind.

The first society hostess to announce her ball actually on the 5 or 6 January held precedence – but woe betide if a greater hostess decided to claim that precedence by making a later announcement for the same date.

A masque ball was the most popular, as it allowed the participants to indulge in the popular eighteenth-century game of Twelfth Night Characters, a game steeped in antiquity dating back to Roman times and before, when master changed places with slave.

In the sixteenth- and seventeenth-century court, excluding the Parliamentary period when all such frivolity was banned, a huge cake was baked with a bean inside. Whoever got the bean in their piece was crowned King of the Bean and ruled supreme for the night. A card drawing game developed in the eighteenth century, whereby each lady drew a card from the box held by a footman to the left of the entrance, and each gentleman drew a card from the same to the right. These cards were caricatures of Pairs. Thus Signor Croakthroat might be paired by Madame Topnote. The guests had to find their partner, and depending on the gaiety of the event, the amount of wine and negus consumed, and the inhibitions of the guests, the character roles had to be taken on in varying degrees of 'spirit' for the whole evening. Signor Croakthroat might, for example, be constantly clearing his throat, and singing musical scales, whilst Madame Topnote

might enjoy making her fellow
guests jump by occasionally
emitting a loud high note!
Stationers were employed to create
exclusive sheets of character cards,
which could not be duplicated at
another party. Those who made the
cheaper sets, which were not
exclusive, kept ledgers of who
bought which set, so that there
were no duplicated embarrassments
for customers.

Jane Austen was known to enter
such activities with more than a
little 'spirit' according to the late
Sir William Heathcote, who is said
to have remembered being with her
at a Twelfth Night party when he
was a small boy. He stated that on
this occasion she had drawn the

Seasonal party at Tredegar House (detail)

character of Mrs Candour, and acted it 'with great appreciation and spirit'.
Mrs Candour would, in fact, have been an ideal character for Jane to
portray. The role involved taking people aside and telling them candidly
what one thought of them, or of their cap and gown, or making outrageous
comments in loud whispers about other guests!

Emma's Christmas

*Prince Regent, later George IV, had a collection of all of Jane's novels in
the libraries of each of his personal residences. His librarian made a
request to Jane that she should write a book, 'an historical romance,
illustrative of the history of the august house of Coburg'. This was
Emma, which Jane dedicated to the Prince Regent, and published in*

1816, a year before Jane's untimely death. As the correspondence relating to this event took place either side of Christmas, perhaps there was an unspoken thought that this should serve as a Christmas gift to the Prince.

To James Stanier Clarke, Monday 11 December 1815

Dear Sir,

My 'Emma' is now so near publication that I feel it right to assure you of my not having forgotten your kind recommendation of an early copy for Carlton House, and that I have Mr Murray's promise of its being sent to His Royal Highness, under cover to you, three days previous to the work being really out. I must make use of this opportunity to thank you, dear Sir, for the very high praise you bestow on my other novels. I am too vain to wish to convince you that you have praised them beyond their merits. My greatest anxiety at present is that this fourth work should not disgrace what was good in the others . . .

As in other novels, Christmas is treated as an oft-longed for event, which, however, on arrival, is often disappointingly low key, almost as if the anticipation of the event was better than the actual event itself. The following extract from Emma *takes place at Hartfield, where after a quietly comfortable few days, the family are faced with a dinner engagement away from home. The contrasting feelings of the party as they prepare for, and finally travel to, the venue for the Christmas Eve dinner party, are as varied and the arguments as accurate as if they were written today of a contemporary 1990s party.*

There could hardly be an happier creature in the world, than Mrs John Knightly, in this short visit to Hartfield, going about every morning among her old acquaintances with her five children, and talking over what she had done every evening with her father and sister. She had nothing to wish otherwise than that the days did not pass so swiftly. It was a delightful visit; – perfect in being much too short.

In general their evenings were less engaged with friends than their mornings: but one complete dinner engagement, and out of the house too,

Letter from Jane Austen to the Prince of Wales's librarian.

there was no avoiding, though at Christmas. Mr Weston would take no denial; they must all dine at Randalls one day; – even Mr Woodhouse was persuaded to think it a possible thing in preference to a division of the party.

How they were all to be conveyed, he would have made a difficulty if he could, but as his son and daughter's carriage and horses were actually at Hartfield, he was not able to make more than a simple question on that head; it hardly amounted to a doubt; nor did it occupy Emma long enough to convince him that they might in one of the carriages find room for Harriet also.

Harriet, Mr Elton, and Mr Knightley, their own especial set, were the only persons invited to meet them; – the hours were to be early, as well as the numbers few; Mr Woodhouse's habits and inclinations being consulted in all things.

The evening before this great event (for it was a very great event that Mr Woodhouse should dine out, on the 24th December) had been spent by Harriet at Hartfield, and she had gone home so much indisposed with a cold, that, but for her own earnest wish to be nursed by Mrs Goddard, Emma would not have allowed her to leave the house. Emma called on her the next day, and found her doom already signed with regard to the Randalls. She was very feverish, and had a bad sore throat: Mrs Goddard was full of care and affection, Mr Perry was talked of, and Harriet herself was too ill and low to resist the authority which excluded her from this delightful engagement, though she could not speak of her loss without many tears . . .

Mr Elton looked all alarm on the occasion, as he exclaimed,

'A sore throat! – I hope not infectious. I hope not of a putrid infectious sort. Has Perry seen her? Indeed you should take care of yourself as well as of your friend. Let me entreat you to run no risks. Why does not Perry see her?'

Emma, who was not really at all frightened herself, tranquillized this excess of apprehension by assurances of Mrs Goddard's experience and care, but as there must still remain a degree of uneasiness which she could not wish to reason away, which she would rather feed and assist than not, she added soon afterwards – as if quite another subject,

'It is so cold, so very cold – and looks and feels so very much like snow, that if it were to any other place or with any other party, I should really try not to go out today – and dissuade my father from venturing, but as he has made up his mind, and does not seem to feel the cold himself, I do not like to interfere, as I know it would be a great disappointment to Mr and Mrs Weston. But upon my word Mr Elton, in your case I should certainly excuse myself. You appear to me a little hoarse already, and when you consider what demand of voice and what fatigues tomorrow will bring, I think it would be no more than common prudence to stay at home and take care of yourself to-night.'

Mr Elton looked as if he did not know very well what answer to make; which was exactly the case, for though very much gratified by the kind care of such a fair lady, and not liking to resist any advice of her's, he had not really the least inclination to give up the visit; – but Emma, too eager and busy in her own previous conceptions and views to hear him impartially, or see him with clear vision, was very well satisfied with his muttering acknowledgement of its being, 'very cold, certainly very cold', and walked on, rejoicing in having extricated him from Randalls, and secured him the power of sending to inquire after Harriet every hour of the evening.

'You do quite right,' said she, 'we will make your apologies to Mr and Mrs Weston.'

But hardly had she spoken, when she found her brother was civilly offering a seat in his carriage, if the weather were Mr Elton's only objection, and Mr Elton actually accepting the offer with such prompt satisfaction. It was a done thing; Mr Elton was to go, and never had his broad handsome face expressed more pleasure than at this moment; never had his smile been stronger, nor his eyes more exulting than when he next looked at her . . .

Mr Woodhouse had so completely made up his mind to the visit, that inspite of the increasing coldness, he seemed to have no idea of shrinking from it, and set forth at last most punctually with his eldest daughter in his own carriage, with less apparent consciousness of the weather than either of the others; too full of the wonder of his own going, and the pleasure it was to afford at Randalls, to see it was cold, and too well wrapt up to feel it. The cold however, was severe; and by the time the second carriage was in motion, a few flakes of snow were finding their way down, and the sky had the appearance of being so overcharged as to want only a milder air to produce a very white world in a very short time.

Emma soon saw that her companion was not in the happiest humour. The preparing and the going abroad in such weather, with the sacrifice of his children after dinner, were evils, were disagreeables at least, which Mr John Knightley did not, by any means, like; he anticipated nothing in the visit that could be at all worth the purchase; and the whole of their drive to the Vicarage was spent by him in expressing his discontent.

'A man', said he, 'must have a very good opinion of himself when he asks people to leave their own fireside, and encounter such a day as this, for the sake of coming to see him. He must think himself a most agreeable fellow; I could not do such a thing. It is the greatest absurdity – Actually snowing at this moment! – The folly of not allowing people to be comfortable at home and the folly of people's not staying comfortably at home when they can! If we were obliged to go out such an evening as this, by any call of duty or business, what hardship we should deem it; – and here are we, probably with rather thinner clothing than usual, setting forward voluntarily, without excuse in defiance of the voice of nature, which tells man, in every thing given to his view of his feelings, to stay at home himself, and keep all under shelter that he can; – here are we setting forward to spend five dull hours in another man's house, with nothing to say or to hear that was not said or heard yesterday, and may not be said and heard again tomorrow. Going in dismal weather, to return probably in worse; – four horses and four servants taken out for nothing but to convey five idle, shivering creatures into colder rooms and worse company than they might have had at home' . . .

'Christmas weather,' observed Mr Elton, 'Quite seasonable; and extremely fortunate we may think ourselves that it did not begin yesterday, and prevent this day's party, which it might very possibly have done, for Mr Woodhouse would hardly have ventured had there been much snow on the ground; but now it is of no consequence. This is quite the season indeed for friendly meetings. At Christmas everybody invites their friends about them, and people think little of even the worst weather. I was snowed up at a friend's house once for a week. Nothing could be pleasanter. I went for only one night, and could not get away until the very next se'nnight.'

Mr John Knightley looked as if he did not comprehend the pleasure, but said only, coolly, 'I cannot wish to be snowed up a week at Randalls.'

At another time Emma might have been amused, but she was too much astonished now at Mr Elton's spirits for other feelings. Harriet seemed quite forgotten in the expectation of a pleasant party.

'We are sure of excellent fires,' continued he, 'and everything in the greatest comfort. Charming people, Mr and Mrs Weston; – Mrs Weston indeed is much beyond praise, and he is exactly what one values, so hospitable and so fond of society; – it will be a small party, but where small parties are select, they are perhaps the

The arrival of Christmas guests, by Randolph Caldicott

most agreeable of any. Mr Weston's dining room does not accommodate more than ten comfortably; and for my part, I would rather, in such circumstances, fall short by two than exceed by two. I think you will agree with me (turning with a soft air to Emma,) I think I shall certainly have your approbation, though Mr Knightley perhaps from being used to the large parties of London, may not quite enter into our feelings.'

'I know nothing of the large parties in London, Sir, I never dine with any body.'

'Indeed! (in a tone of wonder and pity,) I had no idea that the law had been so great a slavery. Well, sir, the time must come when you will be well paid for all this, when you will have little labour and great enjoyment.'

'My first enjoyment,' replied John Knightley, as they passed through the sweepgate, 'will be to find myself safely at Hartfield again.'

Emma *was duly presented to the Prince Regent, and Mr Clarke wrote to confirm this to Jane just before Christmas:*

From James Stanier Clarke, Carlton House, Thursday 21 December 1815

My dear Madam,

The letter you were so obliging to do me the honour of sending, was forwarded to me in Kent, where in a Village, Chiddingstone near Sevenoaks, I have been hiding myself from all the bustle and turmoil – and getting Spirits for a Winter Campaigne – and Strength to stand the sharp knives which many a Shylock is wetting to cut more than a pound of flesh from my heart, on the appearance of 'James the Second'.

On Monday I go to Lord Egremonts at Petworth – where your praises have long been sounded as they ought to be. I shall then look in on the party at the Pavillion for a couple of nights – and return to preach at Park Street Chapel Green St on the Thanksgiving Day.

You were good to send me Emma, – which I in no respect deserved. It is gone to the Prince Regent. I have read only a few pages, which I very much admired there is so much nature – and excellent description of Character in everything you describe.

Pray continue to write, and make all your friends send sketches to help you and Memoires pour servir – as the French term it . . .

I hope to have the honour of sending you James the 2nd when it reaches a second edition: as some few notes may possibly then be added.

Yours dear Madam, very sincerely,
J.S. Clarke.

The same day on which she wrote to the Prince's librarian, she wrote instructions to her publisher regarding the dedication page and advance copy to the Prince. However, even the peerless Jane got it wrong on this occasion!

To John Murray, Hans Place, Monday 11 December 1815

Dear Sir,

As I find that EMMA is advertised for publication as early as Saturday next (16th) I think it best to lose no time in settling all that remains to be settled on the subject, and adopt this method of doing so as involving the smallest tax on your time . . .

The title page must be EMMA, Dedicated by permission to H.R.H. The Prince Regent, and it is my particular wish that one set should be completed and sent to H.R.H. two or three days before the work is generally public.

Sadly I could find no

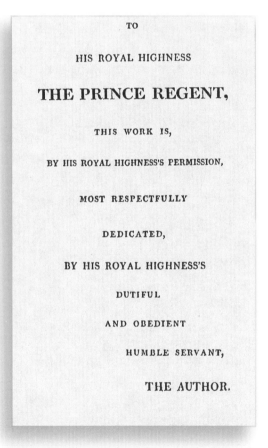

TO

HIS ROYAL HIGHNESS

THE PRINCE REGENT,

THIS WORK IS,

BY HIS ROYAL HIGHNESS'S PERMISSION,

MOST RESPECTFULLY

DEDICATED,

BY HIS ROYAL HIGHNESS'S

DUTIFUL

AND OBEDIENT

HUMBLE SERVANT,

THE AUTHOR.

The dedication page from the original edition of Jane Austen's Emma *trace of the publisher's letter to Jane, but she was obviously put right on the method of setting a dedication, for on the same day she writes again to Mr Murray thus:*

I am much obliged by yours, and very happy to feel everything arranged to our mutual satisfaction. As to my direction about the title page, it was arising from my ignorance only, and from my never having noticed the proper place for a dedication. I thank you for putting me right. Any deviation from what is usually done in such cases is the last thing I should wish for. I feel happy in having a friend to save me from the ill effect of my own blunder.

Parson Holland's Last Christmas

R e v d   W i l l i a m   H o l l a n d

Friday 19 December 1817

Mr Allen past by and enquired after my son. He cannot come down before he is invested in his new promotion on Christmas Day. Now I expected Congratulations on this occasion instead he slightly observed Then he has got his Scholarship. He is made a Student returned I sharply, a Studentship, to all intents and purposes a Fellowship for he can take Offices in the College and succeeds to Livings and it is the Genteelest thing for a young man throughout the University. A little Paultry envious snarling young man, without Preferment himself and yet he cannot bear to hear of such for others. And William he pretends to be fond of. Went to see a strange object at Mr Bennet's. A woman who has neither arms nor legs yet capable with her stumps and mouth of drawing portraits &cc to great perfection. Her parents are poor and lamented much that such an object would be a burden on them but a painter took her and she learned to do things in the perfect manner she does and earns a surprizing quantity of money and maintains the people about her as well as herself. She spoke very well and sensibly.

Thursday 25 December 1817

We had our kitchen full of guests, old Servants &cc and among others the Hero of Waterloo with a Medal, my old Clerk's son. We had a Sacrament this day and many attended and the Congregation at Church was full. I should have observed that many Poor attended for their Donation of wheat. We gave away two bushells which as it sells now at Thirteen shillings a Bushell amounts to something.

Saturday 27 December 1817

My hip still painful at times and my face much so, so there must be something to give a check to our present exultations, no perfect happiness in Life. My children have had a letter from Mrs Yorke congratulating us on my son's advancement to a Studentship but notwithstanding my face pains me. Well so that perfect happiness is obtained at last in another World I must be content with this mixture while here below.

Christmas at Uppercross

Jane Austen

In her last completed novel, Persuasion, *published in 1818, Jane Austen seems to put her own experiences and observations during her stay in Bath to great use. The sparkling delights of that fashionable town contrast strongly with the rather dull Uppercross, much in the same way that Jane must have felt about her final home in Chawton after living in Bath herself. This is expressed in the letter from Mary Musgrove to Anne Elliot, which seems almost a cry from the heart.*

My Dear Anne,

I make no apology for my silence, because I know how little people think of letters in a place such as Bath. You must be a great deal too happy to care for Uppercross, which, as you well know, affords little to write about. We have had a very dull Christmas; Mr and Mrs Musgrove [Mary's parents-in-law] did not have one dinner party all the holidays. I do not reckon the Hayters as anybody. The holidays however, are over at last: I believe that no children have ever had such long ones. I am sure I had not. The house was cleared yesterday except for the little Harvilles; but you will be surprised to hear that they have never gone home. Mrs Harville must be an odd mother to part with them for so long. I do not understand it. They are not at all nice children in my opinion; but Mrs Musgrove seems to like them quite as well as, if not better than, her own grandchildren.

What dreadful weather we have had! It may not be felt in Bath, with your nice pavements; but in the country it is of some consequence. I have not had a creature call on me since the second week in January, except George Hayter, who has been calling much oftener than was welcome. Between ourselves, I think it is a great pity Henrietta did not remain at Lyme as long as Louisa; it would have kept her a little out of her way. The carriage is gone today, to bring Louisa and the Harvilles to-morrow. We are not asked to dine with them, however, till the day after. Mrs Musgrove is so afraid of her being fatigued by the journey, which is not very likely, considering the care that will be taken of her; and it would be much more convenient for me to dine there tomorrow. I am glad you find Mr Elliot so agreeable, and wish I could be acquainted with him too; but I have my usual luck, I am always out of the way when anything desirable is going on; always the last of my family to be noticed. What an immense time Mrs Clay has been staying with Elizabeth! Does she never mean to go away? But perhaps if she were to leave the room vacant we might not be invited. Let me know what you think of this. I do not expect my children to be asked you know. I can leave them at the Great House very well, for a month or six weeks. I have this moment heard the Crofts are going to Bath almost immediately; they think the Admiral gouty. Charles heard it quite by chance: they have not had the civility to give me any notice, or offer to take anything. I do not think they improve at all as neighbours. We see nothing of them, and this is really an instance of great inattention. Charles joins me in love and everything proper.

Yours affectionately, Mary M

The Musgroves' Christmas

Jane Austen

Persuasion *has one of the most vivid accounts of Christmas to be found in all of Jane's novels. Short but most illustrative, here is described the chaos of childish excitement.*

The Musgroves came back to receive their happy boys and girls from school, bringing with them Mrs Harville's little children, to improve the noise of Uppercross, and lessen that of Lyme. Henrietta remained with Louisa; but all the rest of the family were again in their usual quarters.

Lady Russell and Anne paid their compliments to them once, when Anne could not but feel that Uppercross was already quite alive again. Though neither Henrietta, nor Louisa, nor Charles Hayter, nor Captain Wentworth were there, the room presented as strong a contrast as could be wished, to the last state she had seen it in.

Immediately surrounding Mrs Musgrove were the little Harvilles, whom she was sedulously guarding from the tyranny of the two children from the Cottage, expressly arrived to amuse them. On one side was a table, occupied by some chattering girls, cutting up silk and gold paper; and on the other were tressles and trays, bending under the weight of brawn and cold pies, where riotous boys were holding high revel; the whole completed by a roaring Christmas fire, which seemed determined to be heard, in spite of all the noise of the others. Charles and Mary also came in, of course, during their visit; and Mr Musgrove made a point of paying his respects to Lady Russell, and sat down close to her for ten minutes, talking with a very raised voice, but, from the clamour of the children on his knees, generally in vain. It was a fine family-piece.

Anne, judging from her own temperament, would have deemed such a domestic hurricane a bad restorative of the nerves, which Louisa's illness must have so greatly shaken; but Mrs Musgrove, who got Anne near her on

Master among Chidren, by Cecil Aldin

purpose to thank her most cordially, again and again, for all her attentions to them, concluded a short recapitulation of what she had suffered herself, by observing, with a happy glance around the room, that after all she had gone through, nothing was so likely to do her good as a little quiet cheerfulness at home.

Louisa was now recovering apace. Her mother could even think of her being able to join their party at home, before her brothers and sisters went to school again. The Harvilles had promised to come with her and stay at Uppercross, whenever she returned. Captain Wentworth was gone, for the present, to see his brother in Shropshire.

'I hope I shall remember, in future,' said Lady Russell, as soon as they were reseated in the carriage, 'not to call at Uppercross in the Christmas holidays.'

In Olden Times

Sir   Walter   Scott

Of Sir Walter Scott (1771–1832), Jane Austen was said to have 'joked', 'It is not fair, Walter Scott has no business to write novels, because he has Fame and Profit enough as a Poet, and should not be taking the bread out of other people's mouths, – I do not like him, and do not mean to like "Waverley".' However, as his review of Emma *was somewhat critical, if amiable, and her earlier works were described, perhaps tongue in cheek, as 'proclaiming knowledge of the heart', maybe she was just a little put out! Scott's poem is a history of Christmas in microcosm and it was to become an oft-quoted piece of descriptive Christmas.*

Heap on more wood! – the wind is chill;
But let it whistle as it will,
We'll keep our Christmas merry still.

Each age has deemed the new born year
The fittest time for festal cheer:
Even heathen, yet the savage Dane
At Iol more deep the mead did drain;
High on the beach his galleys drew,
And feasted all his pirate crew;
Then in his low and pine built hall,
Where shields and axes decked the wall
They gorged upon the half dressed steer;
Caroused in seas of sable beer
While round in brutal jest were thrown
The half gnawed rib, and marrow-bone;
Or listened all, in grim delight,
While scalds yelled out the joys of fight
Then forth in frenzy would they hie,
While wildly lose their red locks fly,
And dancing round the blazing pile,
They make such barbarous mirth the while
As best might to the mind recall,
The boisterous joys of Odin's hall.

And well our Christian sires of old
Loved when the year its course had rolled,
And brought blithe Christmas back again,
With all his hospitable train.
Domestic and religious rite
Gave honour to the holy night;
On Christmas Eve the bells were rung;
On Christmas Eve the mass was sung;
That only night, in all the year,
Saw the stoled priest the Chalice rear.
The damsel donned her kirtle sheen;
The hall was dressed with holly green;

Forth to the wood did merry men go
To gather in the mistletoe.
Then opened wide the Baron's hall
To vassal, tenant, serf and all;
Power laid his rod of rule aside,
And Ceremony doffed his pride.
The heir, with roses in his shoes,
That night might village partner choose;
The lord, underogating, share
The vulgar game of 'post and pair'.

All hailed, with uncontrolled delight
And general voice, the happy night,
That to the cottage, as the crown,
Brought tidings of salvation down.

The fire, with well-dried logs supplied,
Went roaring up the chimney wide;
The huge hall-table's oaken face,
Scrubbed till it shone the day to grace,
Bore then upon its massive board
No mark to part the squire and lord.
Then was brought in the lusty brawn
By old blue-coated serving man;
Then the grim boar's-head frowned on high.
Crested with bays and rosemary.
Well can the green-garbed ranger tell,
How, when and where the monster fell;
What dogs before his death he tore,
And all the baiting of the boar.
The wassail round in good brown bowls,
Garnished with ribbons, blithely trowls.

There the huge sirloin reeked; hard by
Plum-porridge stood, and Christmas pie;
Nor failed old Scotland to produce
At such high tide, her savoury goose.

Then came the merry masquers in,
And carols roared with blithesome din;
If unmelodious was the song,
It was a hearty note, and strong.

Who lists may in their mumming see
Traces of ancient mystery;
White shirts supplied the masquerade
And smutted cheeks the visors made;
But, oh, what masquers richly dight
Can boast of bosoms half so light!
England was merry England when
Old Christmas brought his sports again,
'Twas Christmas broached the mightiest ale;
'Twas Christmas told the merriest tale;
A Christmas gambol oft could cheer
The poor man's heart through half the year.

A Literary Christmas Dinner

Benjamin Robert Haydon

Haydon (1786–1846) was an artist, better known for his autobiography, published posthumously, which is full of anecdotes relating to his many literary and artistic friends. The following extract relates to a Christmas dinner in 1817, when his guests were Wordsworth, Keats and Lamb.

On December 28th 1817, the immortal dinner came off in my painting room, with 'Jerusalem' towering up behind us as a background. Wordsworth was in fine cue, and we had a glorious set-to – on Homer, Shakespeare, Milton, and Virgil. Lamb got exceedingly merry and

The Immortals. An illustration of literary genius from a scrapbook of unacknowledged
pictures

exquisitely witty; and his fun in the midst of Wordsworth's solemn intonations of oratory was like the sarcasm and wit of the fool in the intervals of Lear's passion. He made a speech and voted me absent, and made them drink my health. 'Now,' said Lamb, 'you old lake poet, you rascally poet, why do you call Voltaire dull?' We all defended Wordsworth, and affirmed there was a state of mind when Voltaire would be dull. 'Well,' said Lamb, 'here's Voltaire – the Messiah of the French nation, and a very proper one too.'

He then, in a strain of humour beyond description, abused me for putting Newton's head into my picture – 'a fellow', said he, 'who believed nothing unless it was as clear as the three sides of a triangle.' And then he and Keats agreed he had destroyed all the poetry of the rainbow by reducing it to prismatic colours. It was impossible to resist him, and we all drank, 'Newton's health, and confusion to mathematics'. It was delightful to see the good humour of Wordsworth in giving in to all our frolics without affectation and laughing as heartily as the rest of us.

By this time, other friends joined, among them poor Ritchie who was going to penetrate by Fezzan to Timbuctoo. I introduced him to all as, 'a gentleman going to Africa', Lamb seemed to take no notice; but all of a sudden he roared out, 'Which is the gentleman we are going to lose?' We then drank the victim's health, in which Ritchie joined.

In the morning of this delightful day a gentleman, a perfect stranger, had called on me. He said he knew my friends had an enthusiasm for Wordsworth and begged I would procure him the happiness of an introduction. He told me he was a comptroller of stamps, and often had correspondence with the poet. I thought it a liberty; but still, as he seemed a gentleman, I told him he might come.

When we retired to tea, we found the comptroller. In introducing him to Wordsworth I forgot to say who he was. After a little time the comptroller looked down, looked up and said to Wordsworth, 'Don't you think, Sir, Milton was a great genius?' Keats looked at me, Wordsworth looked at the comptroller. Lamb who was dozing by the fire, turned round and said, 'Pray sir, did you say Milton was a great genius?' 'No, sir: I asked Mr Wordsworth if he were not.' 'Oh,' said Lamb, 'Then you are a silly fellow.' 'Charles, dear Charles,' said Wordsworth, but Lamb, perfectly innocent of the confusion he had created, was off again by the fire.

After an awful pause, the comptroller said, 'Don't you think Newton was a great genius?' I could not stand it any longer. Keats put his head into my books. Ritchie squeezed in a laugh. Wordsworth seemed asking himself, 'Who is this?' Lamb got up, and taking a candle, said, 'Sir, will you allow me to look at your phrenological development?' He then turned his back on the poor man, and at every question of the comptroller he chaunted:

> Diddle diddle dumpling, my son John
> Went to bed with his breeches on.

The man in office, finding Wordsworth did not know who he was, said in a spasmodic and half-chuckling anticipation of assured victory, 'I have the honour of some correspondence with you, Mr Wordsworth.' 'With me, sir?' said Wordsworth, 'not that I can remember.' 'Don't you sir? I am a comptroller of stamps.' There was a dead silence; the comptroller evidently thinking that was enough. While we were waiting for Wordsworth's reply, Lamb sung out:

> Hey diddle diddle,
> The cat and the fiddle.

'My dear Charles!' said Wordsworth.

> Diddle diddle dumpling my son John

Chaunted Lamb, and then rising, exclaimed, 'Do let me have another look at that gentleman's organs.' Keats and I hurried Lamb into the painting room, shut the door and gave way to inextinguishable laughter. Monkhouse followed and tried to get Lamb away. We went back, but the comptroller was irreconcilable. We soothed and smiled and asked him to supper. He stayed, though his dignity was sore affected. However, being a good natured man, we parted in all good humour, and no ill effects followed.

All the while, until Monkhouse succeeded, we could hear Lamb struggling in the painting room and calling at intervals, 'Who is that fellow? Allow me to see his organs once more.'

It was indeed an immortal evening. Wordsworth's fine intonation as he quoted Milton and Virgil, Keats' eager inspired look, Lamb's quaint sparkle of lambent humour, so speeded the stream of conversation, that in my life I never passed a more delightful time. All our fun was within bounds. Not a word passed that an apostle might not have listened to. It was a night worthy of the Elizabethan age, and my solemn 'Jerusalem' flashing up by the flame of the fire, with Christ hanging over us like a vision, all made up a picture which will long glow upon –

> That inward eye
> Which is the bliss of solitude.

'The Immortal dinner came off in my painting room with "Jerusalem" towering up behind . . .'

Oh Noisesome Bells!

Revd John Skinner

Two entries from the journal of the Somerset rector and antiquary John Skinner (1772–1839), who towards the end of his life seemed to find the joyful bells something of a trial – unlike Parson William Holland, who always seemed to enjoy them.

Thursday 25 December 1823

I cannot say my sleep was disturbed, but my waking hours certainly were by the ringing of bells about seven o'clock, announcing the joyous day, when half the parish at least will be drunk.

Tuesday 25 December 1827

I was awakened early by the ringing of the bells, and could not help thinking how much sound overpowers common sense in all that we have to do in the present day. I lay awake last night thinking of these things, and soon after I had closed my eyes they were opened again by the loud peals these thoughtless people among whom I dwell chose to ring, as they suppose, in honour of the day. They had better retire within themselves, and commune with their hearts, and be still.

New Year Wishes from a Good Aunt

In her last year of life Jane remembered the conundrums and charades of her youth, and wrote a New Year letter to her niece, Cassandra, Charles Austen's daughter, in back-to-front writing. This was nothing so simple as the mirror writing so popular throughout the nineteenth century, but a much trickier method. It appears here as Jane wrote it, with a translation for the faint-hearted underneath!

Chawton,
8 January

Ym raed Yssac,

I hsiw uoy a yppah wen raey. Ruoy xis snisuoc emac ereh yadretsey, dna dah hcae a eceip fo ekac. Siht si elttil Yssac's yadhtrib, dna ehs si eerht sraey dlo. Knarf sah nugeb gninrael Nital. Ew deef eht Nibor yreve gninrom. Yllas netfo seriuqne retfa uoy. Yllas Mahneb sah tog a wen neerg nwog. Teirrah semoc yreve yad ot daer ot Tnua Ardnassac. Doog eyb ym raed Yssac. Tnua Ardnassac sdnes reh tseb evol, dna os ew od lla.

Ruoy etanoitceffa tnua Enaj Netsua

My Dear Cassy,

I wish you a happy new year. Your six cousins came here yesterday and had each a piece of cake. This is little Cassy's birthday and she is three years old. Frank has begun learning Latin. We feed the Robin every morning. Sally often enquires after you. Sally Benham has got a new green gown. Harriet comes every day to read to Aunt Cassandra. Goodbye my dear Cassy. Aunt Cassandra sends her best love, and so we do all.

Your affectionate aunt Jane Austen

December

J o h n   C l a r e

Clare's poetic memoirs describe completely the Christmas of the late Georgian era – he himself was born in 1793 – and show unequivocally the extent to which the Georgians anticipated and enjoyed the Christmas season. The following poem, written in 1827, describes a country Christmas; it contrasts well with the town and society Christmases described in Jane Austen's writings.

Glad Christmas comes, and every hearth
Makes room to give him welcome now,
E'en want will dry its tears in mirth,
And crown him with a holly bough;
Though tramping neath a winter sky,
O'er snowy paths and rimy styles
The housewife sets her spinning by
To bid him welcome with her smiles.

Each house is swept the day before
And windows stuck with evergreens,
The snow is besom'd from the door,
And comfort crowns the cottage scenes.
Gilt holly with its thorny pricks,
And Yew and Box with berries small,
These deck the unused candlesticks,
And pictures hanging by the wall.

Neighbours resume their annual cheer,
Wishing, with smiles and spirits high,
Glad Christmas and a happy year
To every morning passer-by;
Milkmaids their Christmas journeys go,
Accompanied with favour'd swain,
And children pace the crumpling snow,
To taste their granny's cake again.

The shepherd, now no more afraid,
Since custom doth the chance bestow,
Starts up to kiss the giggling maid
Beneath the branch of mistletoe
That neath each cottage beam is seen,
With pearl-like berries shining gay;
The shadow still of what hath been,
Which fashion yearly fades away.

The singing waits, a merry throng,
At early dawn, with simple skill,
Yet imitate the angels' song,
And chant their Christmas ditty
still;
And, midst the storm that dies and
swells
By fits, in humming softly steals
The music of the village bells,
Ringing round their merry peals.

When this is past, a merry crew,
Bedeck'd in masks and ribbons gay,
The 'Morris Dance' their sports renew,
And act their winter evening play.
The clown turn'd king, for penny praise,
Storms with the actors strut and swell;
And Harlequin a laugh to raise,
Wears his hunchback and tinkling bell.

And oft for pence and spicy ale,
With winter nosegays pinn'd before,
The wassail singer tells her tale,
And drawls her Christmas carols o'er.
While 'prentice boy, with ruddy face,
And time-bepowder'd, dancing locks,
From door to door with happy pace,
Runs round to claim his 'Christmas box'.

The block upon the fire is put,
To sanction custom's old desires;
And many a faggot's bands are cut,
For the old farmers' Christmas fires;
Where loud-tongued gladness joins the throng,
And Winter meets the warmth of May,
Till feeling soon the heat too strong,
He rubs his shins and draws away.

While snows the window pane bedim
The fire curls up a sunny charm,
Where creaming o'er the Pitcher's rim,
The flowering ale is set to warm;
Mirth, full of joy as summer bees,
Sits there, its pleasures to impart,
And children, 'tween their parents' knees,
Sings scraps of carols o'er, by heart.

And some, to view the winter weathers,
Climb up the window-seat with glee
Likening the snow to falling feathers,
In fancy's infant ecstasy;
Laughing, with superstitious love,
O'er visions wild that youth supplies,
Of people pulling Geese above,
And keeping Christmas in the skies.

As tho' the homestead trees were drest,
In lieu of snow, with dancing leaves,
As tho' the sun-dried martin's nest,
Instead of ickles hung the eaves,
The children hail the happy day –
As if the snow were April's grass,
And pleas'd as 'neath the warmth of May,
Sport o'er the water, froze to glass.

Thou day of happy sound and mirth,
That long with childish memory stays,
How blest around the cottage hearth
I met thee in my younger days!
Harping, with raptures dreaming joys,
On presents which thy coming found,
The welcome sight of little toys,
The Christmas gift of cousins round:

The wooden horse, with arching head,
Drawn upon wheels around the room,
The gilded coach of gingerbread,
And many colour'd sugar-plums,
Gilt-cover'd books, for pictures sought,
Or stories childhood loves to tell,
With many an urgent promise bought,
To get tomorrow's lesson well;

And many a thing, a minute's sport,
Left broken on the sanded floor,
When we would leave our play, and court
Our parents promises for more.
Tho' manhood bids such raptures die,
And throws such toys aside in vain,
Yet memory loves to turn her eye,
And count past pleasures o'er again.

Around the glowing hearth at night,
The harmless laugh and winter's tale
Go round, while parting friends delight

To toast each other o'er their ale;
The cotter oft with quiet zeal
Will musings o'er his Bible lean;
While in the dark the lovers steal
To kiss and toy behind the screen.

Old customs! Oh! I love the sound,
However simple they may be;
What'er with time hath sanction found,
Is welcome, and is dear to me.
Pride grows above simplicity,
And spurns them from her haughty mind,
And soon the poet's song will be
The only refuge they can find.

Christmas Goes Out in Fine Style

James Henry Leigh Hunt

Hunt was editor of the Examiner *and later the* Refector. *A staunch supporter of Keats, Shelley and Lamb, he published their works frequently. The following is an account of Twelfth Night as he knew it.*

Christmas goes out in fine style – with Twelfth Night. It is a finish worthy of the time. Christmas Day was the morning of the season; New Year's Day the middle of it, or noon; Twelfth Night is the night, brilliant with innumerable planets of Twelfth-cakes. The whole island keeping court; nay all Christendom. All the world are Kings and Queens. Everybody is somebody else; and learns at once to laugh at, and to tolerate, characters different from his own, by enacting them. Cakes, characters, forfeits, lights, theatres, merry rooms, little holiday faces, and last, not least, the painted sugar on the cakes, so bad to eat but so fine to look at, useful because it is perfectly useless except for a sight and a moral – all conspire to throw a giddy splendour over the last night of the season, and to send it to bed in pomp and colours, like a prince . . .

The evening began with such tea as is worth mention, for we never knew anybody make it like the maker. Dr Johnson would have given it his placidest growl of approbation. Then, with piano-forte, violin and violin-cello, came Handel, Mozart and Corelli. Then followed the drawing for king and queen, in order that the 'small infantry' might have their due share of the night, without sitting up too late (for a reasonable 'too-late' is to be allowed once and away.) Then games, of all the received kinds, forgetting no branch of Christmas Customs. And very good extempore blank verse was spoken by some of the Court (for our characters imitated a Court), not unworthy of the wit and dignity of Tom Thumb. Then came supper, and all characters were soon forgotten but the feaster's own; good and lively souls, and festive all, both male and female – with a constellation of the brightest eyes that we had ever seen met together . . .

The bright eyes, the beauty, the good humour, the wine, the wit, the poetry (for we had celebrated wits and poets among us as well as charming women), fused all hearts together in one unceasing round of fancy and laughter, till breakfast – to which we adjourned in a room full of books, the authors of which might almost have been waked up and embodied, to come amongst us. Here, with the bright eyes literally as bright as ever at six o'clock in the morning (we all remarked it) we merged one glorious day into another, as a good omen, (for it was also fine weather though in January); and as luck and our good faith would have it, the door was no sooner opened to let forth the everjoyous visitors, than the trumpets of a regiment quartered in the neighbourhood struck up into the morning air, seeming to blow forth triumphant approbation, and as if they sounded purely to do us honour, and to say, 'You are as early and untired as we'.

Christmas with Mr Darcy

Jane Austen

The much anticipated ball at Netherfield, where Elizabeth clashes with Mr Darcy in Pride and Prejudice, *cannot have taken place very long before Christmas.*

The prospect of the Netherfield ball was extremely agreeable to every female of the family. Mrs Bennet chose to consider it as given in compliment to her eldest daughter, and was particularly flattered by receiving the invitation from Mr Bingley himself, instead of a ceremonious card. Jane pictured to herself a happy evening in the society of her two friends, and the attention of their brother; and Elizabeth thought with pleasure of dancing a great deal with Mr Wickham, and of seeing a confirmation of everything in Mr Darcy's looks and behaviours. The happiness anticipated by Catherine and Lydia, depended less on any single event, or any particular person, for though they each, like Elizabeth, meant to dance half the evening with Mr Wickham, he was by no means the only partner who could satisfy them, and a ball was, at any rate, a ball. And even Mary could assure her family she had no disinclination for it . . .

If there had not been a Netherfield ball to prepare for and talk of, the younger Miss Bennets would have been in a pitiable state by this time, for from the day of the invitation, to the day of the ball, there was such a succession of rain as prevented their walking to Meryton once. No aunt, no officers, no news could be sought after, – the very shoe-roses for Netherfield were got by proxy. Even Elizabeth might have found some trial of her patience in weather which totally suspended the improvement of her acquaintance with Mr Wickham; and nothing less than a dance on Tuesday, could have made such a Friday, Saturday, Sunday and Monday endurable to Kitty and Lydia.

Expecting the dubious but dashing officer, Mr Wickham, Elizabeth was surprised to be engaged for a dance by Mr Darcy himself, not, by his own admission, given to offering himself as a partner easily.

She found herself suddenly addressed by Mr Darcy, who took her so much by surprise in his application for her hand, that, without knowing what she did, she accepted him. He walked away again immediately, and she was left to fret over her own want of presence of mind; Charlotte however tried to console her.

'I dare say you will find him very agreeable.'

'Heaven forbid! – That would be the greatest misfortune of all! – To find a man agreeable whom one is determined to hate! – Do not wish me such an evil!'

When the dancing recommenced, however, and Darcy approached to claim her hand, Charlotte could not help cautioning her in a whisper, not to be a simpleton and allow her fancy for Wickham to make her appear unpleasant in the eyes of a man ten times his consequence. Elizabeth made no answer and took her place in the set, amazed at the dignity to which she was arrived in being allowed to stand opposite to Mr Darcy, and reading her neighbours' looks, their equal amazement in beholding it. They stood for some time without speaking a word; and she began to imagine that their silence was to last through two dances, and at first was resolved not to break it; till suddenly fancying it would be the greater punishment to her partner to oblige him to talk, she made some slight observation on the dance. He replied and was again silent. After a pause of some minutes, she addressed him a second time with 'It is your turn to say something now, Mr Darcy. – I talked about the dance, and you ought to make some kind of remark on the size of the room, or the number of couples.'

He smiled, and assured her that whatever she wished him to say should be said.

'Very well, that reply will do for the present. – Perhaps by and by I may observe that private balls are much pleasanter than public ones. – But now we may be silent.'

'Do you talk by rule then, when you are dancing?'

'Sometimes. One must speak a little you know.

It would look odd to be entirely silent for half-an-hour together, and yet for the advantage of some, conversation ought to be so arranged as that they may have the trouble of saying as little as possible.'

The set country dances of the eighteenth century went through complex patterns and changes, and could last upwards of an hour. By the end of their dance, Elizabeth and Mr Darcy had begun what was to develop into a love–hate relationship for some twelve months. Mr Darcy, however, decides not to keep Christmas in the country, and returns to London, where we are told no more of that season's Christmas amusements, unfortunately, other than a short reference indicating the day had arrived:

On the following Monday, Mrs Bennet had the pleasure of receiving her brother and his wife, who came as usual to spend Christmas at Longbourn . . . The first part of Mrs Gardiner's business on her arrival, was to distribute her presents and describe the newest fashions. When this was done, she had a less active part to play. It became her turn to listen.

After a year of suspense, misunderstandings and reproaches, Elizabeth and Mr Darcy are finally to be married, and it would be pleasant to guess at a Christmas wedding, in view of the letter Elizabeth sends to her aunt, Mrs Gardiner:

I would have thanked you before, my dear aunt, as I ought to have done, for your long, kind, satisfactory, detail of particulars; but to say the truth, I was too cross to write. You supposed more than really existed. But now suppose as much as you chuse; give a loose to your fancy, indulge your imagination in every possible flight that the subject will afford, and unless you believe me actually married, you cannot greatly err. You must write again very soon, and praise him a great deal more than you did in your last. I thank you, again and again, for not going to the Lakes. How could I be so silly as to wish it! Your idea of the ponies is delightful. We will go round the Park every day. I am the happiest creature in the world. Perhaps other people have said so before, but not one with such justice. I am happier even than Jane; she only smiles, I laugh. Mr Darcy sends you all the love in the world, that he can spare from me. You are all to come to Pemberley at Christmas. Yours etc.

ACKNOWLEDGEMENTS

Extracts are from the following:

Jane Austen & her Country House Comedy. W. Helm, 1909
Austen Leigh Private Family Letters. Privately published by the Austen Leigh family 1895 and donated to the Bath Reference Library
Lady Susan. Jane Austen, 1871
Austen Papers. Collated by R.A. Austen Leigh, privately printed and donated to the Bath Municipal Library, 1943
Persuasion, Pride & Prejudice, Mansfield Park, Emma. Jane Austen. John Murray in four volumes, 1818
Charades written by Jane Austen and other members of the Austen family. Private printing, 1895
Sense & Sensibility. Jane Austen, 1811
Jane Austen: Contact with Life, 1904
A Christmas Book. Wyndham Lewis & Heseltine. Dent, 1926
Christmas with the Poets. Collins, 1905
Christmas with the Poets. Vitzelly Bros, 1845
The Sketchbook of Geoffrey Crayon. Washington Irving, 1820
Old Christmas. Washington Irving, 1875
Peter Parley's Tales of Christmas. 1828
The Spirit of the Holly. Mrs Owen. Regency, n.d.
'Letters from England by Don Manuel Alvarez', Robert Southey, 1807
Robert Southey's Letters, ed. Henry Fenwick, 1912
Acting Charades. Brothers Mayhew. Regency, n.d.
Tredegar House in Jane Austen's Day, brochure, 1996

It is difficult to single out one person or institution above another, for all have made invaluable contributions to this book and without them it would not have been written. However, I must first acknowledge my husband, Andrew, who has spent hours chauffeuring, phoning, faxing and proof-reading for me, as well as offering a cheery cuppa along the way! As always, my special thanks go to the staff of Monmouth Library, who have left no stone unturned in tracking down books and references for me; Michael Carter of the Centre for Kentish Studies for his perseverance in finding misplaced documents; Liz Bevan, Valerie Bearn and other staff at Bath Reference Library, whose assistance over several visits was quite invaluable; and Tom Carpenter of the Jane Austen Memorial Trust for all his help and encouragement.

Thanks also go to: Cardiff Reference Library; Humanities Library, University of Wales, Cardiff; Hampshire County Records Office; The Jane Austen Society; Hereford Library; The Pierpoint Morgan Library, USA; David Freeman, Curator, Tredegar House, Newport; and Dionne Johnson of Fremantle Ltd, Cardiff.

PICTURE CREDITS

The author and publisher would like to thank the following for permission to use illustrations:
Jane Austen House Museum (Chawton House Trust), pp. 10, 31, 45, 52, 91
Laing Art Gallery, Newcastle upon Tyne (Tyne & Wear Museums), pp. 56–7
Frances Vallaydon-Pillay, p. 84
Tredegar House/Newport Borough Council, p. 89
The remaining illustrations are from Christmas Archives International

While the author has made every effort to trace the original owners of all the texts and illustrations used, it has not always been possible. In a few cases the most reliable sources have not been able to identify a text or a picture in isolation from its originator. For these few we apologize. If any originators have not been acknowledged here, please write to the author c/o the publisher.

ANSWERS TO CHARADES

No. III – Repeating Watch	No. XIX – Agent
No. IV – Chair	No. XX – Banknote
No. XVIII – Hemlock	